I0132400

Whispers from the Awakening Heart

By Steven Deverel

Awaken Publications
908 3rd Street
Kirkland, Washington 98033

Copyright 2012 by Steven Deverel

All rights reserved, including the right to reproduce this book
or portions thereof in any form without permission.

ISBN 978-0-9885971-0-5

Editing, and layout by MarySue Brooks

Front Cover image "Sunrise on Kauai" by Teresa Deverel

FOREWORD

You are holding a wonderful gift in your hands. At first glance it looks like a book of poetry, but it is so much more than that. It is a book that speaks directly to the inward journey we all are on – the journey from the darkness and confusion of unconsciousness to the joy and clarity of an awakened heart.

I have had the wonderful opportunity to know Steve for a number of years and explore with him the art of opening what has been closed and healing what has been hidden. This book is deeply authentic because Steve knew the shattering of innocence as a child, the despair of disconnection, and the agony of a bruised and battered heart. In his poems, he quietly and beautifully, allows us to see our common heartbreak and invites us to take the journey of healing that is awaiting each one of us.

You may not have known the tortures of boarding school or the disconnect of compulsions, but you too have experienced, in your own way, the broken heartedness which he so clearly describes here. And you, too, will greatly benefit from the wisdom he has gathered on his journey that flows like a golden thread through these poems.

Ultimately, this book is a celebration of what it means to be healed by the very experiences that at first seem to injure. It is also a true and deep celebration of the power of our hearts to reopen to the joy of being truly alive.

~Mary O'Malley

INTRODUCTION

In early 2008, during and after a series of traumatic events in my professional life situation, words emerged which I share here.

I have spent much of my adult life working as a hydrologist. On my 56th birthday, I sat in our company's conference room with a woman whose home in rural northern California neighbored an expanding gold mine. She and her neighbors were concerned about impacts to the creek that flowed near their homes and springs that provided their drinking water supply. They requested a hydrologic evaluation of mining operations of the New Era Gold Mine named after the geologic formation containing the gold.

Some details immediately caught my attention. Noteworthy paradigm shifting events occurred in my life in seven year cycles. So it seemed significant that that this New Era project appeared on the dawning of the 9th 7-year period. On our company's books, this was project number 5555. I was skeptical about numbers representing angelic messages. However, Doreen Virtue's interpretation of this series was fitting: "fasten your seat belt, life changing events are coming". We began work during Easter week 2008. As water is almost always synonymous with controversy in California, adversity was expected, but not at the level experienced.

The New Era Mine received a permit in 1983 to extract relatively small amounts of ore.

With increased gold prices, the mine which had remained semi-dormant for years was expanding. During 2007 and early 2008, sediment transported from denuded acreage and holding ponds clouded creek waters. State regulators ordered the mine to improve the facilities to prevent future violations. The neighborhood coalition requested that the county conduct a new permitting process and environmental analysis. Our hydrologic report indicated potential effects on spring flow.

In late spring, I arrived at the county offices for a hearing before the county board of supervisors. Swarms of mine supporters filled the hearing room. Evidence presented by the neighborhood coalition amidst periodic jeers from the audience clearly demonstrated the necessity for additional analysis and scrutiny. However, the supervisors denied the coalition's request and validated the decades-old permit for continued mining. The neighborhood coalition filed suit under the California Environmental Quality Act requesting an Environmental Impact Report.

The mine owners' attorneys subsequently filed suit against the coalition, our company, the State Department of Conservation and a northern Californian environmental group helping the neighborhood coalition. As I write this, I am reminded of my terror in opening the summons. Our small company, which I had co-founded 11 years earlier, was threatened by corporate bullying. Legal drama ensued for months amidst economic turmoil. Our attorneys nimbly crafted a legal case against what was deemed a strategic lawsuit against public participation and prevailed in court. To this day, a voice mail message from the mining company's attorney remains on my phone. Periodically, I listen and watch my reaction.

From this life challenge, poetry began to flow from an ever-deepening place often devoid of mental noise and judgment. I was touched deeply and experienced an opening of the heart that offered mercy to so many lost and wounded parts of myself that began to merge into a greater sense of wholeness and inner vastness. I shared the poems with others who also were touched. I have found that when we write from a place of inner recovery, we do it for all and thus nourish the process of awakening consciousness which speaks to and opens the common heart: a work in progress and an inside job.

Humans are entering an unparalleled epoch of global awakening. We are called to go beyond the consciousness and actions that resulted in our current predicament. Presence is arising in the midst of chaos and confusion. What we thought were solutions will no longer work. Emerging mercy offers healing and integration at the level of causality. Misguided programs for happiness based on mentally driven physical fixation largely devoid of heartfelt connection with suppressed emotional discomfort are at the root of humanity's dysfunction.

At best, poetry points to the emerging bridge across the chasm between mind and heart. Crossing the bridge is the path forward: the New Era of human evolution. It is a journey which is rarely easy but will take us beyond the grips of the egoic mind which, in its current state, is akin to a torture instrument stealing vital energy. To bring the mind to the heart is bring it into the service of the Divine. This is the true alchemy and the gold of the New Era.

Whispers from the Awakening Heart begins with a chapter containing poems that relate personal experience. "Boarding School," is a metaphor for our collective earthly experience. We are born into a world that is here for us to learn. It represents movement away from the vibrational and emotional realms to becoming transfixed with the material. Through felt homesickness, we return to the Home we never left.

The next chapter, "New Era Gold," offers an alternative to the present-day mind-dominated state of humanity which incessantly seeks the material. Blinded to the futility and consequences, much of humanity attempts to mine earth's immutable loveliness. Meanwhile, many drown in the proliferation of non-essentials and Earth, our home, is poisoned. The first poem, Mining, suggests an alternative source of wealth within and requests reconsideration and remembering. The remaining poems point to the consequences of this mining mentality and an alternate vision and direction.

The next five chapters contain poems describing various aspects of the journey across the chasm; bringing mind into governance by the heart. Poems in Chapter 3 entitled "The Fire" describe the process of entering the consuming fire of present moment awareness. Chapter 4, "Nature's Wisdom," offers poems pointing to the felt security of the natural world and offers a path of surrender.

Poems contained in the next two chapters, "Endearment" and "Work World" explore those elements of the boarding-school experience that most often cause pain and offer opportunities for emotional and spiritual growth; work and relationships. In the following chapter entitled "Unpacking," the poem "The Package," unveils the tightness of human compulsivity held together by a deep sense of faultiness. Remaining poems provide insight into the nature of shame and the process of allowing it to dissolve. The final three chapters contain poems that welcome and remind us of our true eternal nature. The poem "Homecoming" is an invitation to dance, know earth's longing to caress human feet, and embrace our returning to Source.

My prayer is that these poems may assist you on our sacred journey.

For I now know
the preciousness
of few words
arising in silence
and landing like birds
on a tree at dusk;

not mistaken for
but pointing to
the open door.

Time runs out
for worshiping
and scrutinizing
the messengers,
for pouring over the
welcome mat.

Heed and feel vastness and vibration.
Enter curiously and with fascination through
the narrow gate swinging widely
with unbridled anticipation
of reunited creation and Creator.

ACKNOWLEDGEMENTS

I am deeply grateful to all those who inspired
the writing of this book and who have helped
make its publication a reality. I especially
thank my wife Teresa for her loving patience,
attentive ear and encouraging words during
years of weekends spent at the kitchen table
writing poetry. I also thank Mary O'Malley
for her encouragement and advance read and
Mary Sue Brooks for her attentive and loving
care of the manuscript. I extend my grati-
tude to my parents and all those who have
played the often arduous roles of mirrors,
teachers and way-showers without whom the
book would not have been written.

CONTENTS

Whispers from the Awakening Heart

BOARDING SCHOOL

The boarding school experience is forgetting and remembering our belonging to Life as we accept homesickness as the path Home and ancient sorrow transmutes to inner joy. Curiously and mercifully we are called to meet the hurting child-self that left the wonder and innocence of Being to take on heavy mental burdens of rigid intellectual abstractions. Waking to "I am" reveals pieces of the puzzle as Life guides us through discomfort. By sitting with the child-self, spells cast during early experiences are dispelled. Beliefs and stories seem true until we face the walls of separation and allow them to dissolve when touched by compassion. There is no place to go physically or mentally that adds to the Here and Now. This flesh is a schoolroom. When the lessons are learned, we pass on.

Sitting with Dad

on creek bank in foggy terror
as he spoke words of caution and sex,
I froze in the belief that I
was thrust from his house
because I was wrong.

I didn't fit,
banished from his tribe,
too sensitive,
he thinks I belong
at the boarding school.

Why else have you forsaken me
 to the wolves?

For decades after he departed
days before my 14th birthday,
relieved to be rid of me
I believed,
I watched the creek, Life,
flowing past, afraid to enter,
belly tight in the working world,
looking through a mental screen.

Today angels and I sat with him,
offering mercy and breath to tight belly.
Tears flowed joining
with the stream of Life
in the wisdom of the soul's journey.

The Spell

was cast at the boarding school.
I knew I would die shivering
under the covers where I slipped
secretly during the day
even though masters prohibited.

I could not stand in the poison and fever.

Headmaster doctor imposter and wife nurse
banished me to aloneness
in sick bay where bowels moved
like a raging muddy stream and I lay
unable to escape the pain, poop and shame.

Today, sitting with the spellbound
boy on the bed
unravels the spell in seeing
the face of Christ
in the distressed child.

Tears flow to dissolve the spell.

Shrapnel flies reigniting the flame
and the story starts again,
thrusting Little Me
into the spell's net where
mind dwells on others' faults.

So I return to visit merciful light opening
to reveal darkness and shady characters
Little Me wants to think are in others,
but are hidden under the inner bed.
Greedy and fearful fat cat,
terror-stricken complainer and
self-righteous religious;
all feelings in the internal mix
brought into the light.

The Classroom

Rigidity ripples through
children's soft bellies
upon entering the realm
of intellect, control, order and
routine and appropriate behavior.

British masters ridiculed
and berated the homeless
American boy for his
ignorance and poor speech.

Day after day, in dread
he drew near with jaw clenched
and belt strapped hard
around the abdomen holding
breath

in the mist of green
and clear streams
in the Atlantic forest.

Oblivious to the majesty,
he plodded and trudged,
mentally plotting ways
to hide terror and wrongfulness.

He remained for decades
frozen in an adult body
where dread surfaced with
each reminder of the classroom
triggering concealed reflections

and defenses against haunting masters.

An old photo, broken computer,
impending presentation and
time running out forced the

private cerebral casino to hold up
hedged bets for avoiding blame
as places to hide evaporated.

Seeing the classroom from a distance
with whitewashed walls releases courage
to reenter darkness with open heart,
to see the boy and investigate monstrosity,

and curiously on cat's feet,
feel the dark texture of wooden
desks and chairs and close-up
giant faces with cigarette and alcohol
breath, harsh eyes and furrowed brows
spewing so many disheartening words,

and mercifully open to offer heart to the terrified
and behold the face of Christ in hated giants.

Watching, knowing, feeling, welcoming,
Life flows again in stomach cramps unlocking
the holding of lifetimes.

Homesickness

We entered the boarding school and
forgot the joyful truth of running barefoot
on the grass, laughing and silliness,
hugging, holding hands and tenderness.

Rock-like rigidity of formulas,
numbers and words left little room
for playfulness.

Homesickness leads to Home.

It seems too much to bear
and I tried everything I could think
of to become free.

Weeping and waking to "I am,"
each day reveals a piece of
the puzzle at the boarding school
where Life guides through
sweetly laced deep aching homesickness.

The seeming betrayal of a mad world
offers a path through pelvic holding
waiting millennia for liberation.

Curiously exploring,
a small voice answers with relief,
"I desire to return home."
Transcendence, finest seeing,
meet pain monster.

"I see you, I feel you, speak to me."

Ancient sorrow transmutes
to laughing and dancing;
Light emerges from
opening inner flower.

A way clears for mind to return
to heart and
touch eternal consuming fire
to reveal Home never left
where giggling children play in
waterfalls and serene pools
of crystal pure water.

Engage the monster my friends.
Resisting and running away won't work.
Offer mercy, come take tea.

Relax the heart, watch alert,
and alarm not at emanating
harsh and condemning nonsense
of inner urges to expel and suppress.

All flesh shall know this work.

Stroke of Curiosity

Curiously touching belly softness
opened a window to reveal
deep gripping resistance
clutching inner light shaft,
misaligned, off-color.

Terrorized Little One
could not stand
in assault by giants
and cloaked pure alive joy
with armor
holding on for dear life.

It was not safe.

Core imbalance and scoliosis ensued in
seeking without finding.

Then mind recoiled and stopped.

In sacred gap, heart entered,
spaciously allowing,
penetrating, nourishing, awakening
realignment.

My holding is our holding,
fuel for light
rising in the spine
for prayer and communion.

Boy in the Chevrolet

Car sped over a bump
when I was five.
Whee! This is fun.
Body felt alive.

Words emerged. Penis tickles.
"God hates that..." came on mother's fiery
breath.
Beneath her control, joy submerged.
Silence engulfed like death.

Heavy metal doors shut both ways.
Little boy froze, nowhere to hide.
He remained rigid inside the Chevrolet.
So much hinged on words spoken by

monster morphed from pretty mother,
(she was the life source),
suturing shame and sex together,
followed by years of pain and strife;
so much nausea during car rides.

Voices shouting shield from more hurt,
images of rapid thrusting flash.
You are such a failure they blurt.
Harsh words on my stomach crash.

Today in back seat I ride.
So much mental noise called
to open heart,
voices subside.

Primordial Sound

During pre-dawn awakening to
tissue stretched across abdominal anvil
I mentally repeated
it is alright that you are here
yet also disputing, why is this still here?

Mind approached hardness
and bounced away.

Sleep drifted in and out amidst
tintinnabulation in the bones.
Thoughts floated like fire flies
flickering and disappearing into darkness.

Amidst curiosity on a rolling sea
of floating sensations,
the veil parted to expose
a little boy alone
on a deserted suburban street,
unbearable pain,
rocking,
holding stomach,
hard edges inside and out.

The thin place revealed
so many unseen decisions
by the hidden duo,
child with pain
and mind locked
like fist in
"pain be gone."

Pain cannot leave
without taking the child.
Life requests mercy not sacrifice.
What remains unseen controls.

Fluid primordial sound:
timbre of flowing water,
geese in winter sky,
songs of angels and happy children,
pulse in the marrow and
pour tender mercy
so deeply needed ,
yet never before received.
Stay as long as you want.

Boy on the Grass

Curiously penetrating the body's
layers of time, I found him
sitting on the lawn squeezed by harsh edges;
manicured grass against leveled and squared
speckled concrete sidewalk and gutter,
flush on stinging black asphalt.

He sat alone writhing, holding the gut
on abandoned suburban street,
neighbors peering through dark windows,
parents absent.

I sat at his side watching, not
needing change;
hard edges softened.

Palms rested on cool soft green,
shaded by mighty sycamore, gentle leaves
lightly dusted with white powder.
Cracked and weathered brittle bark,

like pieces of a puzzle, dropped away
to reveal the naked trunk of new beginnings
and a glimpse of immutable beauty
sustaining the journey home.

At first he resisted and retreated to a dark hole.
Then, his hand reached above the void,
joined with mine while still clinging,
mostly in the hole, limp.

Later, he leaped into my arms.

Silently inquisitive about the sense of things
in that room in my house that was once closed
by a door tightly shut with a sign reading
"Danger, do not enter,"

I give attention to the once-lost boy.

More and more, he from that place and I
from mine,
we cross the chasm between pain and mind.

Who cries?

I
In distant mirror I smiled,
winking at the boy with broken
teeth on the school playground,
frozen,
blood draining through feet
into the redwood bark amidst
melody of school children
running, jumping, laughing,
swinging from steel bars.

Deaf to the music of Life,
wrongfulness solidified
in hearing words
"You are so ugly."

He learned to hide.
Alone among classmates,
he did not smile
and furrow on the brow deepened;
corners of the mouth
turned further downward.

Until inner vulnerability
like a soft newborn,
still preserved yet locked away for
decades, opened the door in
softened belly and entered sunlight
to reveal itchiness of new beginnings.

II

To what do I owe this visit?
What is to learn?

So many failed requests for love.

A final picture smiling with
broken teeth before the closing
shared with fiancé and placed
in the first picture album
next to her pretty smiling perfect teeth;

couldn't she at last make that ugliness
disappear and the boy feel lovable?

All the while it was an inside job.

Reaching through the mirror to sit
with boy on the rough redwood board
next to bark that so often fell into clothes
and crept up the legs;
itchiness ensued for hours;
belly and mental fist tightening
around need to scratch.

Face down, his sobbing became my own.

III

Who is crying?

Contorted face, upper lip curled,
desperate naked one calls
it personal and unjust,
phantom fanged inner beast
slowly unglues to reveal light shining
through the eyes of the vulnerable lamb
compassionately holding suffering.

With arm around bony shoulders
that at such a young age already
carried too much weight,
he looked up and smiled,

face shining like the sun.

Battered teeth from face-first falls
and lunging fists and feet
finally died and gave way
to smiling and speaking once more.

"It is fine that you are here;"
insides finally turned out to reveal
eternal inner smile.

The Story

that appeared shining and true
for so long unravels and loses luster
in light of eyes graced by
the anvil of pain.

It is the story of the rigid hero
caught in the rock-hard double bind
written from Life's crippling blows that
force us to ask for help.

I really do not want
to walk this path of suffering,
but you see,
I must do Life alone because
I am not worthy to receive.

Yet there it is in the chest,
the glowing heart space where
preciousness dwells and now reveals
itself in the midst of angelic safety.

This is True help for all,
gathering lost lambs
dispelling the story.

Tears emerge from rigidity
that says that it has been too long,
and heart closes again and

I cannot let go of the story;
the wall is rock solid.
It cannot be torn down;
I can't break free.

You cannot, dearest little one.
We can.

Presence creeps through tortuous
undercurrents and shines light on
pretentious honor and dignity,
rendering even the most solid
monuments of human pride.

Allow the wall to be touched by
Compassion, and behold it crumbles.
It was never real.

Faded Photographs

revealed college friends;
serious faces hiding pain and fear,
and glowing smirks grasping
narrow-necked bottles of beer.

Athletes for the Alma Mater,
who in disdain
ran in circles,
lifting and squatting,
trudging legendary circuit,
pulling and pushing.

Weeks after news of divorce,
home dissolved,
squish,
acid pressure,
ruptured disc,
ruptured foundation in
deeply locked and hidden belief that
I was to blame.

"Stop swimming," Doctor said,

"No!" I cried.

Aqueous safety like fluid spirit caresses,
carries timbre of loveliness
taking the shape of any vessel contained,
giving life to all living things without striving.
Water flows to places humans reject and
obeying not human laws, goes where it wills
joyfully frolicking and splashing,

silent, deep still.

Alone in the water for hours,
terror of asking for help and rejection
of looking in the mirror
escaped.

Faded photographs awakened shame
for not knowing,
for drinking to ease the pain.

I met the lost "me" from then,
the one driven to do it all,
still part of my flesh,
tension of misguided searching,
and offered heart and forgiving embrace.

Through Aloneness

I arrived at the here and now
and connectedness.

It lasted for long enough.
I did not trust life and lived alone in the attic.

"Please do not bother me."
I ventured down the stairs enough to feel:
too painful to open locked doors
with signs that read "Danger, do not enter."

So I lived alone even with others;
I lived alone.

Then came the double bind:
hurting children inside and out
desiring freedom.

When heart closes,
all are objects of the mind.

Broken open one day
with little girl's words
through clear eyes;
"You are hurting."

Light came in through cranial crack
with some freedom to face
the pain in the house that became
too much to carry,
like heavy trunks full of wet garbage.

Opening to hell takes us beyond hell
into vastness of Being.

First came aloneness: so many hours sitting
on tractor parked in the yard,
sojourning in the head to avoid terror;
toddler wandering about without a place,
unable to express.

Cerebral traveling comes to an end.
No place left to go that adds to
the Here and Now where
fellow sojourners become
subjects of the heart.

NEW ERA GOLD

Mining is our inheritance. It is emblematic of seeking wealth from a fear-based belief that there can never be enough and I am not enough. The result is struggling with Life, which causes pain and suffering. Children suffer in the neglectful and manipulative mental prison created in the mad search for more. The mind, gripped by ego, tortures. Pain of separateness spawns perceived needs to compensate for felt wrongfulness. Our futile attempts to control our surroundings open to remembering that our Essence is wealth. Life asks us to turn, see, and remember mercifulness and tenderness, to watch the judge that declares unworthiness and bring the mind to serve Love's desire. Liberation of a hidden and trapped child self within all of us nourishes the process of awakening. Atonement with our Source is the path forward.

Mining

flows through my ancestors' veins.
Pain of aloneness transcends generations;
fathers distant from mothers and children
desire closeness yet know not the way.

Miners seek riches found within
the pain-shrouded heart,
the true mother lode,
stillness beneath "if-only" mind.

Extracting scraps of metal happiness
is a hard way to live.

Children await loving embrace, but
miners know not what they do.
Engraved scripts play again and again
as mind clings like a battered child reaching
for an abusive parent.

Sweat-covered faces,
torsos smeared with red dirt
carry loads of ore.
Wild eyes betray terror,
"Will there ever be enough?"
"I am not enough!"

Beyond mind madly seeking more,
pregnant with inner wealth,
true worth lies.

Touched by Alchemist,

pain of holding transmutes,
mercifully revealing treasure
hidden for millennia.

Grace rains on lost moments
reunited in forgiveness.

Time for mining slips away
as earth's creatures slowly drown
in proliferation of so many non-essentials,
and joy eludes.

In her immutable loveliness,
from the heart of the
womb, Earth respectfully requests,
"Turn, see, remember."

The Little Girl

appeared in a dream.
I inquired as I stepped
from a desk full of papers,
did she prefer a walk or a story?

She chose the story as
her tiny hand gently gripped
my index finger
and warmed my heart.

The story began before Grandma,
but she was the earliest one I knew
to be caught in the spell.

Her father was a miner.

I felt her adoration in stories, faded
pictures and letters written during
mostly separate lives.

My heart wept and
tears flowed in my core
upon reading elegant manuscript
littered with "must" and "should."

He thought he knew that she
somehow needed to be perfect.

So the story passed through generations:
men lost in the head and serious business,
unable to see and feel the pain.

Sons, daughters, mothers
carried wounding of millennia
and sought relief from felt faultiness.

Pain of separation requests:
"Turn and look within."

In this, burdens ease as we remember
tenderness and mercy
in the Essence of who we are.

A Vision

came upon hearing,
"This is the lamb of God
that takes away the sin of the world."

Visceral doors opened to release
inner Wellspring;
Love freely given and received;
children emerged to partake in the feast.

Lightning surged in the body;
earlobes lit on fire,

Enter the Kingdom.

We knew before the mind thought it knew;
we are one with the earth and its creatures;
soft body aliveness recognized
Life as celebration.

We stopped trusting when giants
showed us we were wrong and
we fearfully entered mental distraction
thoughtfully removed from Life Now,
while lambs hid in rooms
we dared not enter.

Lost children veiled in pain
courageously arise
to fully feel and read the Braille
and traverse the abyss
between mind and heart
for benefit of all sentient beings.

One Man's Surrender

transmuted torture device meting out
pain, confinement and abandonment,
into symbol for the Divine;
teaching through extreme example.

"If-only" mind gripped by ego,
always wanting something beyond
what Life offers Now,
tyrannizes and tortures,
isolates and confines
in avalanches of desire and hellish resistance,
and drags humans on a torrential
river of mayhem.

Greater desire –
Greater suffering.

Follow the way of surrender
to surely end this seemingly
endless inner war.
Offer each day into the care of our Source.

Sit in sacred stillness.
Stand in, welcome the pain.
Sink into armored aching heart space
protecting holding of lifetimes.

Even in hell, open heart.

Live not in the room of fear.
We deserve better accommodations.
Feel Life's intensity in fearless knowing
that we may not live out this day.

Abandon self completely,
one piece at a time.
Surrender harsh mental cruelty

bearing down in darkness
to float in pure still awareness.
Let it all in. So much fearful holding
brought to heart to break mind's
neediness.

Hasten slowly.
There is not one moment to spare.
Breathe each precious breath fully
in the great Ahhh.
Live in the hot fire of Now,
leaving no trace.

Wait not for the other to open heart.
Work with what is given.
Fully embrace brokenness.
Dare to love unconditionally.
Gaze into the Beloved's eyes
once and for all.

There is no thing to lose.

Each moment lived fully
is an entire lifetime.

Pretentious honor and dignity will
give way to honoring Presence.

To serve Love's desires,
return mind to heart.

All Judgment is Self-Judgment

It began with fellow worker;
resentment seethed for so long.
What needs to be seen?

Meditating, sleeping, waking,
the awaiting voice spoke,
"How could you be so stupid?"
One by one, all decisions
were judged idiotic.

Like the recurrent dream
in the classroom, unprepared
yet unable to leave,
visceral tightness arose.

I peered through
to see gentle Little One hidden,
waiting to know acceptance
without the need to be smart
or appear so.

Tears flowed as this awareness
arose from inner sobs
and convulsions
to reveal this theme throughout.

No one seemed untouched, yet
all were never really affected
by the judge that
declared them wrong.

All are divine help to find and give
space to this innocent exquisiteness
that lights the heart from within.

Volume is loud and pain great.
We have run out of time

to not hear, feel and see.

Make straight the path.
Allow the armor that
barricades the heart to fall away.

Valleys will fill and hills flatten
as mind crosses the great chasm
to the heart.

Atonement

Resplendent with purity and wonder,
wetlands, forests and Life's creatures,
violated, poisoned and mined,
the Great Sacred Womb desires oneness
with earth's daughters and sons.

She is hurting and proclaims:
"You are one with this.
Return, awake
to share in my pain.
Offer heart as vehicle to
transmute cosmic suffering to joy."

Water flows to purify.
Holy breath sweeps
through the body of humanity
in the depths of woundedness,
touching with infinite mercy
rumblings and grumblings
that seek to rise and condemn,
releasing unforgiveness.

Childhood brokenness mends
and integrates "me" and "mine"
into "we" and "ours"
as I see Presence in you and you in I.

THE FIRE

The soul's journey always seems to return to the Kitchen where the fire is hot and people congregate to help us grow. Felt perception of discomfort triggered by people and events is the fire of the here and now fueled by the trapped energy of suppressed childhood emotions. Every irritating one is self-forgiveness knocking, offering a mirror to help us find and gather the lost sheep separated from the fold.

The fire burns deep within, hollowing out egocentricity, cleansing roots of fear. Entering this inner pain is a liberating adventure in which holding relaxes into grassy fields where lilies open in anticipation of the coming spring. Alert attentiveness to perceived separateness allows Presence to dissolve the mortar of shame that holds bricks of pain.

Every time a crisis comes and we open rather than close, we are liberated and mental models unfreeze. Blindly, step by step, we cross the chasm to the heart where all children receive homage of the wise.

The Kitchen

I recall words in grandma's kitchen:
 "no matter where guests go,
they seem to like my kitchen best."

Why does the soul's journey
always return to the kitchen?
Fire burns hot there and
acquaintances congregate,
smoking their drama,
eating too much desert,
trying to quench the heat.

God knows Grandma saw her
share of drunken attempts to avoid
flames of pain.

Guests oblivious to the soul's wisdom
in sojourning towards awakening
rearrange furniture,
create separate space and
offer unsolicited advice,
enter fear and interfere
while their pain grows unattended.

Then Life serves up something
not on the mental menu.

Descend from attic
and cross my friends and
rejoin to feel the moment,
fuel for the fire that frees the soul,
burning through holdings
stirred with conscious, curious exploring.

All becomes one for greater humanity.

More words in Grandma's kitchen:
"God grant me the serenity to accept
the things I cannot change,
the courage to change the things
I can, and the wisdom
to know the difference."

Today, when once-again caught in the spell,
words on the refrigerator penetrate the heart
of the matter:

"Do you prefer to be right or happy?"

The Fire Burns

deep within
hollowing out.

Can you feel the heat while
curiously exploring and gazing inward
 NOW?

Open heart to our pain and
know it as fire burning for all
without consuming what is Real;
transforming illusion into light;
burning through resistance to Life,
releasing holding for merging with
the fire deep in the belly.

Allow it to burn intensely
to see and feel the way home.

Desperation

I visited thin primordial stillness,
pulsating breath resonating in the marrow.
Deep in the void, an adolescent exclaimed
"Help!"
In the echo, tingling orgasmic
joy welled up and engulfed.

In still aftermath,
exploring in resistance,
a soft voice spoke.
"Place your hands on the table,"
and oh, my God,
underneath so many children cowered,
squeezed by desperation that
says, "Perform and conform or perish."

The tight ball of tender flesh cries out
for Friendliness and Compassion
to know relief in "I do not do alone."
Yet it stirs, convulses and groans
like an injured animal
as I reach to gently touch and feel.

I will not hurt you.
I commit to be with you,
to feel your pain
underneath the barricade.

Softening, striving and toiling of breathless
tightness
relaxes into grassy fields where
lilies open excitedly yet ever so slightly
in anticipation of the coming spring
emerging from the dark and cold winter
dream

to know strength of elephants
and peace of doves and rest
at the altar in the heart
forever undefiled where all illusions
are stripped naked.

Amidst the clamor of voices that cry,
"No we cannot," we stand transparent
in the storm that dissolves the wall
of pain and shame to wake from
the fiction comma.

Blindly, step by step,
we cross the mind-made chasm
to the manger of the heart
where all children receive
homage of the wise.

I stood

in the inner wall curiously exploring
bricks of pain and mortar of shame
created from the threadbare belief
in separation.

Embedded friends want release
from the story of betrayal
held by "Little Me" mind that desired
trustworthy companionship
and received rejection.

I saw a small blue light
deep in the belly
wanting to come home.

The story falls away as
this tiniest of lights shining
from within begins to dissolve
the wall that wants to protect
this elegant loveliness from
hurls of an insane world.

The Table

We came indoors from wild adventure,
wonder of smell and Life between our toes,
to hide under the table;

a carved massive wood structure
with spotless white linen
covering children in the solar plexus;

like a filing cabinet categorizing souls, flesh
and minds.

Life is never enough there
where hands grasp soap bubbles
in fear of death.
The numbers grew,
squeezed by dogma and ideology.

Little ones long to emerge and know
freedom from bondage to express
true creativity.

The mind cannot stand
hurt again and again.
Mercilessly it sits above
trapped little ones.

A dream showed me the way.
My home was next to the church
and in the distance, the river
where I longed to be apart.

Then I sobbed naked in the vestibule
lying with the Beloved.

Waking, I sat with them
under the table in the solar plexus
light filtered from the heart space.

Today I sit breathing in eternal fire
that burns under the table,
curiously releasing
brothers and sisters,
to the wisdom of the soul.

What if

every irritating one
is self-forgiveness knocking?
The angry, or sullen silent one,
or the incessant talker; all offer
a choice.

What does "if-only" mind require?
Go away, shut up, apologize?

To allow Life to release needs
from cerebral fist, go in and in and in.

An obnoxiously self-righteous one
entered my space and would not leave
despite my desire that it be so.

In the midst of mental twisting
around the facts of the case,
convincing mental jury to declare
him guilty and me innocent,
the pain became too great.

I prayed for release and from some small
silence
between complaints, I heard the finest heart
whisper,

"He, too, is my child."

Thoughts unwatched and believed
infinitely separate
heaven and earth and
choke the heart with armor
and encrustations.

Tearfully cerebrally cracked
and brought to my knees,

I beheld obnoxious self-righteousness
as mine,
hidden, toxic, covering desperation.

I thank him for playing the arduous role
of way-shower hand-picked by Presence.

Once cast from closed heart,
I welcomed us and a gate opened.
Two beings became one in the heart,
each using the other as mirror to
uncover holdings and fear.

We need all the help we can get.

To find and gather the lost ones
separated from the fold,
travel down the dark staircase,
step by step, feeling the Braille,
blindly holding the hand rail
into the white purifying fire.

Breath Fire

pulsating through root hairs of fear
and cleansing umbilical cords to shame,

burning what is no longer needed,
liberating, touching not the Real.

Fire burns in the bush of eternal Life,
but the bush is not consumed.

Nothing real can be threatened.

Softly, we tread on holy ground
where only the warm ashes of fear
remain.

Life on the Mountain

On the second day of solitary trek,
I longed to explore the forest,
first the waterfall then the summit.

I forgot to ask for Life's direction.
In infinite wisdom and mercy,
the Universe gifted me.

Darkness, water and trail elusive,
dehydrated, fever, chills, headache,
pulse racing, left me unable
to leave the wilderness.

That night I sat alone in holding.
Mind wanted to create emergency.

They directed me; I heard them.

"Loosen the belly, dear child,"
tight jaw and shoulders, headache,
all connect to the abdomen
gripping and resisting ancient discomfort.

Slowing receiving with each breath softening
tissue, loosening flesh, clenching pain,
mercifully
allowing, welcoming,
aliveness flowed
through and through.

In receiving pain, we touched fire,
rejoiced and entered Holy rest.

Dawn came and I returned
from the mountain,
one step at a time, joyfully weeping.

THE WISDOM OF NATURE

Entering nature in alert stillness reveals Life's dance. Love is freely given through every blade of grass, naked branch, and eddy of water directing us to our inner preciousness and channeling support for the journey to wholeness. Fiercely, nature tears at the fabric of our lives, opening hearts to seeing what is Real. Death is surrender to transformation in remembering that all things pass away in this amazing play of form.

Dancing

As the sun set, I noticed him.
His silent gaze from perch
on ditch berm met mine.

He looked to burrows on road bank,
spherical head rotating freely
on noble shoulders,
wide alert eyes returned to watch me.

For several minutes we gazed.

Suddenly he crouched, lifted and flew
circling overhead, goldenness
merged with diffuse illumination.

He sang; melodic screeching requested
avoidance of young ones in the burrow,
or perhaps declared that to live is to dance.

As his body glided effortlessly,
I beheld the dance;
beyond this human merging briefly
with golden burrowing owl,

extending across green fields
to the mountains, swallows swirling,
cotton tails hopping,
all one dance.

How does one enter this dance?

Only one thing is needed:
watch in stillness with beginner's mind,
let thoughts float in open heart space
like butterflies in the mountain meadow
and fireflies flickering and fading into
nothingness.

Openly receive each moment
and you will know freedom.

Not easy.

Easier than you think.
Hold not to freeze-dried mental models
that imprison the soul and obscure
the Dance of Life Now.

Let heart flow to what it needs.
Feel life directly.
You already know.

An Answer

Puppies dance about the house
and yard, celebrating, wrestling,
singing and stirring it up.
They chew at the fabric of our life,
ripping papers, tearing cloth.

I laugh; she does not think it is funny
and tells me so.
Stormy weather is required.

Words can only point to the joy
of the chase, tackle and tumble, smiles
and prancing with the trophy (a stick),
heads held high.

They are Spirit incarnate,
humorously opening our hearts
to what is Real.
This I think is an answer.

Allow the fabric to tear and
the winds of grace to blow through
in the midst of messiness.
Step into the grace-filled dance.

In deep stillness,
all Creation shouts for joy.

Retreat to the Creek

Finding peace passing city limits,
I retreated to watch the winter sun
find rest behind the mountains.

Yellow organics sifted through the
tangled leafless branches
while creek moved in its bed;
delicate wind chimes amid
voices of angels,
tintinnabulation,
penetrate the heart assuring
a human home among
loving trees and caressing waters.

Help flowed as tearfully I doubted
and knew every blade of grass,
naked branch and eddy as love freely given.
A diamond became visible in the chest
and life suddenly fascinated;

joy of being in love with all that is.

Mind cannot fathom and
mental noise subsides
to allow knowing of Infinite Intelligence,
soft emanations of peace emerging from
milieu.

You may theorize and conceptualize
how all this works, but I have never felt
Presence from hunching over these
gross approximations of the truth
felt in lying on a forest floor
sinking into grace.

Cups runneth over with information,
but we know only a little.

Sunrise on Kauai

We rose before dawn to see
the day unfold at the beach.
Cool sand mingled with naked toes.

It began at the edges where
billowing clouds meet the sea
to reveal ever-changing light
in violet hue, and then more
and more light ignited the clouds.

We watched awestruck with crabs
next to their index-finger holes,
black pin-head eyes gazing west then east
as earth received and gave purple
and orange light.

Awaiting mountain forests glowed.

Blazing inception sent sweet jubilation
through bodies, and tears welled from
the depths of earth bowing to
this life-sustaining illuminating
reflection of One Animating Presence.

The Dragon Fly

Nature seems cruel today.

Small black, wiry cat
captured dragon fly
and with gentle mandibular hold
pranced into the house.

He and large, lazy, orange tabby
cat who came to life jumped with
gentle creature and played into death.

Paws batted like soccer players
throwing airborne
fine lace translucent wings humming
rhythmically, futilely attempting escape.

Vibrant green body once soared
in garden and blue sky
slowly stretching wings,
eye-filled head scanned the landscape.
A finer flying vessel is difficult to find.

Cats rested with legs outstretched, watching
as it lay fading in last flailing movements.

Greif is here reminding
of frightening lost touch
with original wondrous nature,
remembering all things pass away
in this amazing play of form.

The Rat

arrived at the back door.

Mo the cat, intrepid hunter,
gently and proudly held in feline jaws,
released seemingly lifeless fury form
that then jumped like a kangaroo
into the bushes with Mo in hot pursuit.

Later, rat lay alone
near death
on welcome mat,
brown and gray fur
bloodstained,
eyes like slits,
each breath
more distant
from the next.

I knelt and stroked soft fur
during few remaining breaths,
deep and stretching snow white belly
evermore scarcely visible,
like breath within breath.

I barely noticed
last breath come and go,
hoping for yet one more,
I mistook my breath for his.

Alas, his belly rose yet not again
and he lay peacefully motionless with
tiny legs outstretched and paws softly folded
as if signaling readiness to receive.

I wept, thanking
for showing the way to surrender:
to live, run and die without
struggle and grasping.

Dusk

arrived in the mountain meadow where
delicate white dandelions nestle among Corn
Lilly.
Golden glow remained on the blue crumpled
and
crushed rocks of the west-facing slopes.

In waning light, I followed the deer path
behind the willows; cool airy moistness
greeted me in stillness.

In an instant, I saw her sitting in the grass.
I froze and she took flight, revealing at
my feet four tiny blue spotted eggs
safely held in the brown straw nest.

In an instant, my lungs emptied and I
saw for what seems like
the first time ever in human history,
Life itself in raw splendor.

In an instant, I knew I must retreat.
I was the intruder into this sacred
and fragile space.

To linger, mentally label and gawk
meant thwarting this tender show of
Life:
eggs needing mother's warmth.

In an instant I was gone.
In that instant, I truly saw.

Egret

in grassy field without buildings,
with red and white sign
declaring "Space Available,"

waits, watches, slowly and fluidly walks,
deliberately and graciously
thrusting her head forward
followed by slender white flame
of a body extending and contracting
on legs like bamboo stilts.

Driving by on nearby street,
you would not likely notice her
looking for food in recently
mowed spring grass drying and yellowing.

Like lightening, she thrusts her beak,
retracting field mouse trembling
in abject terror, black gravel eyes popping
in yellow orange blades.

She throws back her head, nodding
on slender snake-like neck
as in grateful laughter,
fur quivering in her throat.

These things we call life and death
are not as they seem, I think.

To separate life from death is to
separate mind
protecting some thing
from heart.

The time will arrive,
perhaps sooner than we desire,
for our departure from earthly habitation of
physical fixation.

Clinging to no thing,
we now know enough to willingly
run and dance in celebration one day,
finishing business moment to moment, and
enter the next into the humorous softness of
the white eternal flame of loving embrace
as we are lifted from this human form.

No need to second guess.
Hold back not the heart.

Trust the leaving as so precious.

Open Fields

At sunrise we crossed the road
to puppy Promised Land.
They strained at lead while I gently
ushered them to heel, and
they lunged forward again and again
like mental impulses
returning to the guidance
of the Watcher.

Finally arriving at this Field of Dreams,
they saw the great egret still,
watching golden straw for a morsel.

Puppies, released to run, chased
white stillness lifted to circle overhead
on slow gracefully flapping wings.
She floated and toyed and they followed;
earth rising to meet their outstretched paws,
springing airborne,
contracting and expanding
muscles glistening in early sunlight
propelling them across the land.

How they love to run and give joy to watch.

The egret roosted in the pine tree
like a cloaked priest and watched over the two
pressing their noses to the ground,
sniffing every inch for God knows what.

The For Sale sign disappeared
from this open field
and soon I think machines will come
to remove golden straw
and grind and trample

the gray cracked soil.

Soon, puppies, I, hawk, egret, will perhaps
find other open fields in which to play.

A Fish Jumped

Beyond structure and ordered municipality
I sat at the still pond where setting
winter sun peered through naked trees
whose inner calm is undisturbed
and deeply rooted in warm earth.

It was not long since their leaves were
on fire and swept away as they stood boldly
in the cold north wind.

A fish jumped a few yards from my seat
on the wet clay bank, and
silvery light reflected in the setting sun
shot to my heart
where I saw the littlest boy loving Life,
wanting peace in the midst
of turbulence and fighting.

Breathing into messy space
where sickness and tightness in doing
prevailed,
I awakened to trust Life emanating from
ordered chaos and temporary forms.

The light sends an urgent message
into the artificial human matrix
where mind tries to extract trustworthiness
and safety from temporary forms that
 bugs and rust consume.

Hear this ancient plea:
enter the darkness,
embrace the wounding,
allow light to shine
from inside out.

Geese Honking

in the winter sky
resound like joyful voices of children,
music in the midst of superhuman feats
of strength, endurance and selflessness.

Life among humans could be so,
joyfully striving together,
mercy at hard edges,
relieving neighbors' brokenness and fatigue,
primordial sound penetrating
and relaxing in the marrow,
nourishing awakening.

We have only to offer ourselves to love
what the soft gentle animal inside us loves.

Alone on the Mountain

Desperate tension of aloneness
dwelled in the gut
with desire to cry
and run to noise and
end self-imposed banishment.

In resistance fully felt and allowed,
tears welled and flowed within
showering subtle joy.

Butterflies danced in celebration
in the meadow floating apart
and reuniting and then apart again,
motion defied intellect,
Creation animated as if by
great Bunraku puppeteers.

The psalmist wrote,
"Angels camp with us."
I can't see them.

I can feel Presence.
in still space as
trees, ants, birds, butterflies
sing "be here now" and channel support
for our journey to wholeness.

Thanksgiving Day on the Big Island

lingered from the beginning.

Restlessly desiring exploration,
I went to the beach
to sit and watch pink and violet clouds
gently usher goldenness into distant silky
darkness,
and black crabs on black lava rock
receive from cyclical swelling
as the aqueous womb spread a foaming
white table cloth on polished rock which
then returned to the source to reveal

joyous ballerinas with tiny gravel eyes
thankfully lifted,
as fine-pointed legs carried them sideways,
to capture essential tidbits.

I did not notice an unknown friend approach
from the bosom of nearby family gathering
with plastic yellow plate in hand with
carefully placed turkey slices
next to stuffing and ladled gravy on potatoes.

Suddenly he appeared to present the gift,
and words of gratitude released from my lips
fell upon his silent turning to rejoin his clan.

So I think this is how it can be:
attentively and gratefully receive
and dance, dance like the crabs.

Lone Pine

Alone in the wilderness, fear rose like
terrifying mallet in dusk's waning light
and heart began to close when,
upon seeing doe in meadow, opened
to awesome spacious safety.

Stealthily I approached,
bare soles eased into
cool delicious wet grass
and black mud.

Curiously she looked and allowed as,
on haunches, I watched her peacefully graze
and daylight wane to indigo and full moon.

Earth received me in infinite
secure bosom as I lay on the knoll
overlooking the meadow in
soft moonlit still grandeur.

Twistedness in an ever changing world,
years of mental spinning and grasping
to escape core-gripping,
deep heart-wrenching grief
avoided since infancy and felt fully then
in bitter aching
and sweetly-laced immutable loveliness
and deep flow of Being emerging
within and through nearby lone pine tree.

A dwarf, also with bent and twisted trunk,
steadfastly stood without mental suffering.

Needle fingers lovingly extended
to embrace meadow's wet richness
and meandering cool crystal clear streams,
lone pine expressed Presence gracefully
before my resting place,
teaching.

ENDEARMENT

Relationships offer great opportunity for awakening. Most enter relationships pretentiously, bartering in the joining to keep Life at bay and live a safe and controlled little piece of life. Inside things grow and fester and we often find ourselves camping in the valley of quiet desperation. Pain arising from relationship conflicts knocks at mind's door silently screaming, "Feel me, and let me in."

To allow the heart to merge with the painful tightness is to know the glory of the playground and see and feel precious light in ourselves and those around us. We can give only love, for this is who we are. Truly, intelligence infinitely more than mind can fathom, brings us together to face what sometimes looks like hell, allows it to transmute to Life and grants illuminating adventurous freedom.

Terms of Endearment

We bartered in our joining:
 I will make you happy
and in gratitude
you will express your happiness.

In this way we keep Life at bay
and live the safe and controlled
little piece of life for a time.

Inside, things grow and fester.

Deep inner voices clamor unworthiness:
"If I can't please, I can't live."

Shady characters
gather and multiply in
unseen dark corners,
plundering the heart.

Harshness flows forward to
awaken the pain monster.

Old mind grows tired of niceties,
cuteness, anger and rejection.
Shame comes to roost and
we camp in the valley
of quiet desperation.

When pain is too great
and backs are against the wall,
light shines through a cranial hairline crack
to reveal the chaos,
requiring surrender to the mess.

Tight armor that covered heart for centuries
begins to tearfully and rebelliously
relinquish its little throne
to the light of our seeing.

The ever-changing belly,
center of self-crucifixion
and resurrection,
contracts and expands as
mind tries again and again
to play God.

To allow the heart to merge
with tightness is to know
the glory of the playground,
fullness in living with feet firmly
planted on the welcoming earth
and receiving arms outstretched
knowing that we can give
only love for this is who we are.

Twice Already Today

harsh words came
flashing from the depths.
"No, I can do it,"
three times repeated
before cock crowed.

Waking from the nightmare,
frozen thoracic heaviness emerged.
I tried to cover and think,
"How could this happen?"

How infantile.
Pensive heaviness
strangled life's flow.

This is old ground
hardened by drought,
crying to be known,
craving refreshing rain of attention.

Knocking at the door of mind
it silently screams, "Feel me, let me in.
Give me space.
I come to be part of your life."

"It is ok that you are here," I say
to the familiar abdominal rigidity.

Really, I would rather it would leave,
evaporate, or be magically removed by
Some Higher Power.
Believe me, I have prayed for this.

It recedes for a time.
Then like a foreigner
it appears.

Smoke from the fire,
when the wind shifts,
blinds.

It seeks to divide what love holds.

Yet, during interludes I look
into her brown eyes that lead
deep into Preciousness and
I see the child I have known forever.
Laugher explodes from between her teeth.

Even when her face contracts
in victimhood and fatigue,
I can see into eternity.

I glimpse healing surrender today,
cherishing these lost lambs within
and bringing then into the fold.

Sweet Sorrow Flowing Heart

News of anomalous mammogram spurred
spinning story of losing you.

I followed to a deep purifying place,
meandering in the sweet grieving sorrow
and nameless heart-aching heaviness,
then gratefully returned to Present
flowing one Heart,
remembering
no thing is that important.

Then the blood-test results came
again thrusting me into deeply
seeing old unsettled accounts.

Lying together during pre-dawn,
I feel pain greater than your pain
or my pain.

It is our pain.

Plumbing into visceral holding
and reservoir of grief,

I breathed life into lifeless children
deep within,
fearfully gripping hara line
strangling life flow in terror
of falling into the abyss.

Anguish of a lifetime is here
for reconciliation, as all
accounts cancel
and grief fully felt
burns its way
to the heart.

Thanksgiving

Look. Trees turn to fire and light
gracefully welcoming winter;
take our foliage and we will rest.

Listen. Gaggles of geese navigate heroically
and precisely in the twilight sky,
honking wildly and purposefully,
primordial sound resonating
in human marrow.

It was my father's favorite season.

On many Thanksgiving days,
he led his children
through the neighborhood of his youth.

With spring in his step, he told stories.
I remember as if I was there
during the War amid unspoken terror,
delivering newspapers,
surrounded by lifelong friends,
playing games, wining a yo-yo contest.

He taught us much, but
no greater lesson than
surrender.

He traveled the world
working in many foreign lands.
In early November of his 79th year,
he returned home in a wheel chair.

On his final Thanksgiving Day,
his fading body lay
in my sister's home
where the picture of
sailboat on still water hangs.

Silently I watched
heaving chest.
Yah,
breath entered over deep throat fluid,
emerging through open mouth;
Weh...
Yah Weh...
Yah Weh.

I looked at bodily changes
to avoid seeing and feeling
(blue fingers, gaping mouth
grasping at breath
like a fish out of water).

Eyes closed, labor-pain laden words emerged
 "Oh God",
then
"Ok, surrender",
a word I never heard him say.
He softened and heart sighed.

He gripped my hand.
From the depths of
stepping towards eternity,
and returning,
practicing death,
he woke me.
His face radiated Light,
 "Hi ya" .

I saw what I truly loved,
and knew forgiveness
and finished business
in a young boy, wild,

fascinated with Life
hidden for so many years.

A few more hours he remained;
soon after dusk
he passed.
I hoped for one more breath.

Yah Weh.

Perfumed Presence filled the room
where sailboat on dark, still water
remained.

In contrived glumness, two dark-suited men
emerged from darkness engulfing the body
in a black plastic bag.

Efficiently zipped and removed,
space remained
surrounding a plastic red rose
laid on the pillow.

I stepped into the night and sat numb,
watching the crumpled black bag move
across the lawn from the gurney
into the hearse
and disappear.

Surprised by the depth of my grief
which emptied wails from my chest
into the cold black night,
mind cried,
"We were to have more time."

The gentle Presence of that holy
"hi-ya" instant gracefully

touched grief with the knowing
that this is the way of things,
this form I idolized is gone.

Shared spirit larger than life
dwells within,
gently touching terror,
fearful mind that knows
we are not the form
but cannot fathom that we
are Something Else.

Fear that when death comes for me, like
immobilizing cold stone on the legs,
it will find me arguing,
uttering, "Oh shit,"
turning from the light,
holding to illusion,
building more barns to fill
before allowing rest.

Thanksgiving today
is the gift of simple words:
"Ok, surrender,"
to enormous Evershinning
in us all;
just this much for now.

Finger of God

Teresopolis, Teresa's city,
rests at the feet of dappled gray mountains
majestically protruding
from Brazil's Atlantic Forest.

The highest peak surges to explore its
own height, smiling upon clouds
of unspeakable softness;
Dedo de Deus,
Finger of God.

As a child thrust from my father's tribe,
I lived there at the British school.

Sons and daughters of man suffer at the
hands of elders. Old ideas, "should"
and "should not"
transfer heavy mental burdens to little ones
that become too heavy to carry
and drop of their own weight.

Joyous memories
shine through time.

Fugitive from hard edges,
the soft animal within found
amazement running bare back
in cavernous friendliness
of the bamboo forest,
splashing naked in clear pure
mountain streams,
tasting the wild sweetness
of guava, pears and sugar cane.

I know the indomitable spirit
of fellow students,
who in the face of severed family bonds

and torn ethereal flesh, so often responded
to the words "Go to hell" with,
"I am already here."

In the neighboring state,
a girl named Teresa
dreamed of living in America.
We met ten years later.

She glanced through her smile
from across the room,
head thrown slightly back,
captivating with happy nobility.
We married within a year.

Children from opposite hemispheres,
Presence handpicked us for each other.

Unsure how to pray,
I watch the emerging
pieces of the puzzle,
and this I know:

the finger of God and all its entourage,
infinitely more than little mind can fathom,
holds hell surrounding it like sunlight
and transmutes it to Life,
granting illuminating adventurous freedom.

Censorship

Little Me always wanted peace,
you know how that goes.

On my terms please,
which I do not express
because I know you
will dislike me or laugh.
Please read my mind
or do as I silently
and forcefully do,
or else silent scorn
or good bye.

It started with the earliest memory.

Not to bore you with my story, but
there was so much pain.
That part always seems the same;
perhaps it will help you in your journey.

He covered his ears to shut out fighting
and hurt, but toxic milieu flowed in
to settle the jaw, and he believed
it was something he did or said.

For over a half a century he froze
between green tile hospital walls
surrounded by strangers with masks
that removed his organs.

He, too, took on the mask,
afraid to come home and
speak his truth

until decay took up residence
in the mandibular prison
while Presence and Open Heart

mercifully entered the enclave and mind's
fist began to open.

Cautiously removing the mask allowed
tears to flood through heart to dissolve
contorted face with tight lips
that so often met the world with
"No, really, I am fine."

Welcome home, little Dear One,
speak your truth.

Images of Motherhood

Divine images from nature:
fountain of life
offers tenderness, mercy, protection
and shelter to young ones.

Like the mother duck
swimming with ducklings in tow,
and bear shielding her cubs,
love is offered freely to
infants that know peace in
maternal embrace,

beauty and wonder pointing
to ever-present inner fullness.

I am here for you always
reminding that you are expressions of
The One Life.

So it is with the open heart.
Hold your self and all beings
as beloved children.

Give freely as you have freely received.

Celebration

The parish hall is dark, empty and silent.
Fluorescent lights transform shadows
to stacked portable tables which unfold
to take on plastic yellow with blue flowers.

Produce waits at the back door.
Volunteers crowded into kitchen
busily chop, mix and cook for
this community meal. Guests arrive.

The tall, broad-shouldered man found work
after searching for two years.
Surprised, woman with chapped red
swollen hands, hugs, tears rise.
Grateful gaunt man says
it's the only meal today.

Trays brim and travel to tables
amidst happy melodies flowing from
gray bearded man's fingers gliding
deftly over piano keys and
agile female companion with wide
blue animated eyes, singing, playing
violin and tap dancing.

Life's expressions move within vast sacred
musical space.

In our garden, tomato plants stand tall,
clinging to galvanized cages above
flowing cucumber and water melon.
Grape vines wildly stream on the fence.

Delicate lavender and sage grow
in a separate place where bees congregate.

Each one flowers and bears fruit
at the required time as we come to know
our Essence as wealth.

Where the fences meet, Alchemist
receives and transforms what remains
in the compost pile at the end of the season.

WORK WORLD

The world of work is rich with opportunity for growth. It is where the action is, where the rubber meets the road and friction generates heat. The economic crisis brought us closer to the fire in the belly – great Presence in the midst of apparent loss. We have worked compulsively, grasping for more. Certainly this upheaval has come to clean us out for new adventure. Angelic Presence offers tools for opening the wellspring—breath, curiosity, mercy, space and body awareness—so we may know peace in working with our brothers and sisters.

As we curiously explore Life moving through work, programs for happiness taken on by delicate juvenile psyches come to light, revealing misguided motivations. Poems relate causal investigations of present-day resentments and reactions, insidious tentacle-like mental reaching for more, and attempts to control life. Much psychic glue holds a panicked child-self firmly in place deep in the basement. In facing terror, we come to know peaceful relief in letting go of professional burdens.

Surrender is the only way. This is Life today and "I don't know" is fine as I rest in the tangled tenseness giving stones space to shift. Presence cares deeply to help us see. Enlightened doing is the path forward. We live among doubters needing to see and feel the wounds in order to surrender the need to be right and seek fulfillment in a mad world. Light flows through a heart-sent message of salvation and oneness with the earth through facts emerging unobstructed by making someone wrong.

Tools

We traveled an adventurous path
next to deep water through grassy fields,
pants and boots soaked with delicious dew,
to discover that on that cool spring morning
I went to the job site and forgot my tools.

The fire-haired angel brought her tools
and opened the well.

She woke me.
Stay awake that you may endure the test.

Of course,
to meet my brothers and sisters,
I need tools to free the watcher
of the story of betrayal and desperate
wanting for affection by little
abandoned one in frozen aloneness.

Angelic Presence in the
Heart space spoke:

We offer tools to reopen the well,
Great Source of Sustenance,
time after time:
breath, curiosity,
softening hardened tissue,
mercy for little ones,
space for angry ones
that fear, defend and
want to fight.

Thankfully inhabit the body.

Offer clear cool water to those in need.
There is plenty to drink for yourself as
you are nourished in the giving.

And so I met my brothers and sisters,
and we found peace never lost.

Edges

Humans persist in creating seemingly
hard edges and rigid boundaries.

Illusion and pain.

Pure awareness is edgeless;
all dissolves in Ultimate Mystery.

Sit and quiet the mind.

Can you feel while gazing
upon so many right angles
the slightest deep tightness
crying in darkness amidst
mental chattering?

Surrender in the great letting go
"Aah" breath.

Explore the compulsion wanting
to create more edges to grasp and hold
as "me-mind" tries to manage the infinite.

Confronted with awesome majesty,
we, like Peter, are compelled to
build tents around the edgeless,
that which cannot be enclosed.

Beloved,
Life, offering pieces of the puzzle
for our delight, is well pleased.

The unexpected or unwanted takes us
to the edge of our pain dissolving
at the frontiers of merciful attention.

Resistance desires to fall into Being
through the window of the human heart.

There is something useful here
in gently ushering mind into Being and
letting it back again, to see answers and
feel truth at barricades and boundaries,
back and forth.

Let no thing go unexamined.
All is wanting and waiting to be seen.

January 2009

Late Friday afternoon they came,
emails and calls,
"Stop work," first one project
then another.

Grasping for breath.
"This is it, we are doomed."
It is just the beginning.

Later in silent darkness, I saw
fire in the belly.
I went close, retreated and
approached again.

Great Presence in the midst of loss.
I have always worked.
Time has come to serve.

Wealth Flows

In the midst of economic turmoil,
I recalled brazen college friend,
Nitche (maybe not his real name).
His sports car careened through darkened
Berkeley streets; they called him insane.

He chanted a mantra:
"Money follow money,
money do follow money."

A freshman from the suburbs,
visitor from another planet
to that city by San Francisco Bay,
I listened to the streetwise, and perhaps
absorbed wisdom in my naiveté.

Give too much attention to the news and
worry and fear become prayer, blocking
flow from source to need.

The sad and hidden blame game
gives wealth away to the misguided one
with no financial skills and leaves us lame.

Stop sending messages to the Universe:
"Gifts are not welcome here,"
for what is given is received.

To have all, give all to all
one by one:
allow wealth to flow like blood
to nourish the Body.

For long enough we have bought the lie
we are saved by what we buy.

In Presence, a little is all that is needed.

In "little me" mind, having every thing
is never enough.

As old mind grows tired of struggle,
weary of holding and grasping,
hunching over glowing screens to protect
the strangled heart,
it fades like a sleepy aging dog.

Faced with surmounting chaos,
former victims lead, fresh and new,
showing the way through knowing
we are in this together.

Surely upheaval has come to
clean us out for new adventure.

I think soon we will smile and say,
when businesses closed,
we opened our hearts
to seeing our Essence as wealth.
Easily and without strife, wealth flowed.

The Little Worker

It started with resentments in the workplace
(big surprise!);
such a persistent and curious package carried
for decades.

And then the little worker showed himself.

He saw no place for himself, and
walked softly so as not to anger
pretty mother and win the affection
of busy father rarely present.

He took on household tasks
that mother, often ill, could not,
in desperate efforts to create peace
and find acceptance in the family of man.

He picked up toys,
cleaned the floor,
stood by father's side
and imitated his work;
hid in the doghouse
or crawl space when all efforts
failed to bring peace longed for
and instead created more
tightness and anger that
persisted to this day.

And on this day,
I went to sit on the sofa
in the messy living room
where Little One was still trying
to make peace by gathering
and storing the clutter.
I invited him to sit,
and he relaxed for a time,

relieved to see and be seen.

He resisted and cried,
 "I do not want to come home;
I want to love but cannot trust."

You are troubled and anxious
about many things.
Let us relax, enjoy,
serve with undivided heart.
This is the better part
and will not be removed.

I Will Show Them

They (the world I suppose)
left me to be alone and
Little Me was terrified for so long,
excluded from Life.

So the cerebral story went
which sought unfolding
in showing them that I am
worthy of their attention.

But alas, once received,
the story was never complete;
such emptiness.

The world teaches to seek love
but not find;
no one that loves Little Me
is worthy of love.

Life became the incessant ebb and flow
of doing and trying to please, tension and
compulsion: a hard way to live.

Hard as the hammer used to bludgeon
brothers and sisters with
Little Me's facts and correctness.

Today is the first day of the week.

I sit in the yard receiving
cool spring breeze on my cheeks.
Puppy nose gently touches my feet
offering occasional wet kiss.
Roses exquisitely sway.

The landscape is green
with excitement and possibilities.

Panic

Exam thoughts lead to tightening.
Who is here?

I am so alone.

If I can only pass,
I will not feel terror of aloneness,
others will not look down upon me.

Despite countless hours of study
at grandmother's mahogany desk,
I may not know enough,
and then failure, again, alone.

This is why the Little One panics.

Is there another way?

Greet and offer space
in the heart of hearts.

So much psychic glue holds
the panicked one firmly
deep in the basement
crouched in the corner,
alone.

The student at the new high school
studies alone in his room,
lusting to alleviate pain of aloneness,
looking out the window
at the empty suburban street
across the manicured lawn,
dreaming of escape and adventure.

Sobbing.

Come up the stairway and
join in the true adventure.
Pass or no pass,
be as rich as you need to be.

Desire

Trembling hands reach for future and
grasp at mental images.
Soon busy mind is weeks away and
tight bellied body pines to follow.

Tentacles reach from heart space,
searching for relief from
loveless emptiness of the cave.

Mind spins and toils with possibilities.
Will we get the job?
We surely are best qualified.
God knows we deserve.

Yet as more mental noise ensues and
days linger without answer,
Little One inside resigns.

Victimhood, shame and jealousy push
the stone tighter at the mouth of the cave
closing the heart.

Little mind tries to control Life,
all the while sending divisive messages
into the wilderness of the business world.

Desire, octopus-like tentacles
extending from the center of the chest,
desperately seeks work as savior even
in latent awareness that
deadlines will emerge
like looming tornados ready
to disrupt life's peaceful evolving.

Again and again stepping back,
surrender is the only way.

This is Life today.

"I don't know" is fine and resting
in the tangled tenseness of the heart space
gives the stone a little space to shift.

The Lawsuit

Knees weakened and gut hardened in terror
as shaking hands opened the manila envelope.

The return addressee awoke the pain monster
who gobbled accusations on numbered lines,
pages laced with fear
from lawyers representing the mine.

Pressing into the heart space,
I queried.

From darkness
a boy timidly emerged
innocent yet accused,
gripped by the neck.

He sought refuge
masquerading as the perfect one,
avoiding father's
angry hand and eyes,
arising from nowhere,
blindsiding again and again.

Welcome.
Thank you
for being here.
I am here for you.

Wrongfulness

Litigation shrapnel flies;
they have no case,
but continue to hedge and pry.

Settlement offer arrived
like a church altar call,
accusing with questions and demands;
confess and promise
no future dealings with those folk.

You are not qualified!

Gasping and raw,
eternal wrongfulness felt,
like dozens of voices
shouting unworthiness
from heads thrust into the belly.

Who are you?
I am here for you.

I bore crumbling, frightened inner phantom
trying hard to appear right,
needing attention.

Allowing and feeling all this
felt suddenly right;
just enough Rightness
holding wrongfulness,

like woman folding into flour,
yeast from the dark fetid recesses.
Monumental corruption
brought to right measure of wholeness.

Tight aching faultiness surged
asking for more curiosity,

revealed
Father's disappointed face
merged with lawyer
sternly saying,
"Oh for Pete's sake."

Loosening grip of mind's fist,
breathing, opening
one finger at a time
into the heart space,
twisted wad opened slightly
to reveal a golden spark within,
energy flows throughout.

Wrongfulness II

Little Me believed it could trust;
a deal could offer relief from
expensive legal drama.

Wrong again.

More insults hurled,
spiked fists to the solar plexus,
deeper than before,
personal yet impersonal.

Lawyers looked for anything amiss
in boastful righteousness.

Breath left
amid tightening aloneness,
no one to trust,
face contorted in agony.

What is revealed in this?

So much energy spent
proving others wrong and
little mind right.

Mental committee reprimands,
strips me naked and raw.

Surprise,
terror loosens,
let it be so,
peaceful relief.

Tiny spark eclipsed
by thoracic terror,
emerged and broadened,
settling turbulent mind.

Then arose more mind stuff;
maybe poetry and prose will
make me famous and well loved.

Who resists precious solace of Anonymity
that accepts Identity from Life unfolding
Now?

Grief holds father's last days,
uttering for the first time,
"Surrender."

Light in the midst of heaviness
carried to the end.

Let go now of trying to be someone,
do something, control Life's flow.

Surrender.

Let hell-creating calcified
mental models float
in merciful awareness
without grasping for more.

Self-image begins to melt;
Spaciousness emerges to
experience the vastness of
what is.

The Article

Giver plays;
stirring it up,
shining light
on warped lines.

Today it was my article
absent from publication.

They promised.
Some email malfunction impeded
transmission of corrected
galley proof.

Editor exclaimed,
"This never happened before."

Abandonment and rejection felt
because of a few missing words
for me to watch the alchemy;
showering inner tears,
tightness loosening,
releasing joyous lightening
through and through.

Presence cares deeply
to help me see.

This Cannot Be Threatened

Traveling to the workshop, I remembered
my imagined betrayer would be there,
and then came the grip in the gut.

Not new.

Voices emerged expounding his defects,
spewing names.

Awareness came from the place
that knows, with heartfelt reassurance,
a Safety that cannot be threatened.

This is real.
Our inheritance.

Mind appears to squander
with useless thinking and
pain-avoiding acquisition

this Safety that can be
only temporarily forgotten.

The Business Deal

They came to buy us out.
A lot of money says Little Me
who sees greed, tension, rush and drama
and calls it personal and fears
captivity of craziness.

Little mind says work is for me
to feel wanted and happy,
remove feelings of uselessness.

This never worked.

Two sides of the same coin;
desire says it needs
and fear says it can't work
for the Corporation.

Feel and watch.

Release the old held
since first days on the job.

Die a thousand deaths each day
and live.

One way through.
What does Love ask?
Rest in "I don't know."

Heaven and hell dissolve
into Spaciousness where there
is room for all, even confusion.

Mistaken Identity

Poetic words calm and open
inner hardness
to words flowing from resistance;

I just wanted friendship, admiration,
confidence and companionship.

Colleagues and superiors were
Daddy surrogates,
strong, hard working.

But then impatience and anger came
fooling me again.
This did not deter trying
everything to earn a loving
and look for any exit
reacting from so much anxiety.

I wanted Daddy to recognize goodness
manifest in accomplishments.

The unearthed memory
from the British School
helped me listen, feel and see.
It was first holiday
during Easter Week.

My father drove the jeep
on treacherous mountain roads.

In sleepless anticipation,
I watched headlights
move during pre-dawn.

There was so much to say to
unavailability.
Hunger remained unnourished.

What did I do wrong Daddy?
Tentacles of desire reached,
please tell me that I am not garbage
to be thrown from the home
where my brother and sister live.

Yet he could not and the tentacles
searched elsewhere,
heart closed in "I cannot trust."

Resistance dogged every step.
Little mind will not go
where it fears rejection,
so it rejects before being rejected.

I see and feel.
It is fine that you are here.
Let tentacles rest.

Please

In that familiar thin place the voice
from deep in rear basement
proclaimed to the engineers,
 "please do not reject me."

Dad's face appears
often in my work.

Inherited rejection is stored
furthest from the mind.

Years of walking on egg shells
like a timid mouse,
leaning forward,
pelvis recoiling from Life,
turning away from emotions
wreaks havoc on hips and back.
Hurting feet proclaim
I cannot stand this.

The "me" hurts and
prefers aloneness in the attic.
while the pain in the ass
begs for attention.

Primordial fear went astray
deep in the guts tightly
imagining future confrontation
and work challenges.

This October day is cold,
wet and blustery,
but Fire burns
in heart so spacious
that lovingly caresses
"please do not reject me."

The Conference Talk

The conference approached and
terror came in waves
of fear worse than death;
voices claim stupidity.

Keep this hidden in stuffed feelings of
the Little One that stood so nervously
in front of the class at the new school,
hands thrusts into denim pockets,
staring at the floor, shifting from foot to foot,
thorax soaked with sweat, mind paralyzed.

Such felt shame in being seen and
not having read the book,
All Quiet on the Western Front.
Teacher probed and prodded;
no place to run.

Black crows cawed in the stomach
held in place by belief in
"I don't belong;"
tremendous effort expended to
sequester and appear in control
while crows flap about
seeking any exit.

Mind retreats to the safety of
dessert and distraction
in the den where voices grow louder
until I mercifully listen and proclaim,
you have a right to be here.

I felt the lost one at the British School
berated for poor speech (enunciate, enunciate!),
humiliated
tears held back
in the midst of belittling.

Offering mercy,
inviting Presence,
that little one turned
beautiful lifted face,
and life flowed
through darkness.

Crows took flight and became doves.

The Invitation

An interesting puzzle emerged;
random phone call,
thoughts of working in Brazil,
and then came the invitation.

Such accolade and honor for little worker;
finally recognition deserved.

Mind raced like torrential river
through projected topics and explanations.

Look what I can do and have done;
amazing the audience with wit
and extraordinary native language skills.

He wants redemption and desires mercy
for so much toiling to show
that he is not garbage
to be tossed from the home.

Seeing the story,
light flows through an opening
to guide heart-sent message
of salvation and oneness with the earth
through facts emerging unobstructed
by making someone else wrong.

For we live among doubters
needing to see and feel the wounds
to surrender the need to be right and
seek fulfillment in a mad world.

Give freely as you have freely received.

UNPACKING

Unpacking is ego undoing. Faced with unbearable loss, heart cries out and touches mind, "we are out of time," and light filters through torn fabric.

We become teachable, open to the notion that this pain and suffering are integral to the tightly held package of self that begs to be unwrapped, letting Giver in through just a little space for curiosity, Now.

Shame is the glue, illusory and slippery, that says, "I am wrongfulness." Welcoming this timid tiniest little entity deep within to the heart, we do for the benefit of all. Terror stored for lifetimes dwells next to thoracic angelic loveliness—Presence desiring wholeness. They encounter like reluctant lovers stealing away to rest blindly in embrace, penetrating deeper into releasing the tightened fist of resisting mind, one finger at a time.

Waking, we offer mercy to all aspects of the suffering self.

The Beginning

Faced with unbearable loss,
heart cries out,
touches mind,
gently grabbing shirt collar,
speaking softly yet firmly,

"we are out of time."

The pain and insanity
are just too much.
I wish not to return again.

Light filters through
a tear in the fabric
revealing inner landscape overrun
with chaos and corruption.

Busy mind paused and stopped trying
to think the way out.

I allowed myself dis-ease
and became teachable.
Ego-puncturing wound allows
toxicity to drain.

The great journey across the chasm
between heart and mind begins;
what mind set asunder,
heart begins to mend.

The Package

I want to surrender,
but God won't remove
this hideous compulsion.

It is a package, my friend,
that contains the life situation
masquerading as Life,
tightly bound and separate.

Work, relationships,
future looking, grasping,
suffering,
package and holder
resist Life Now.

Deep within, out of sight,
fractured pieces of the mirror
lie blanketed by shame
where compulsion hides in the story
we must do life alone,
cannot trust, and
blame self and world for wrongs
within and without.

(Surely no other mind can be as crazy as mine).

"If only" mind spins,
toils and reaches,
rarely fulfilled,
barricading the heart.

God honors our choices and
does not intrude.
Responsibility and freedom
are the same.

Disconnected from Now,

weary and anxious,
pressure seeks relief
in the face of unbearable hurt
and engages lust as a way
to sedate and control Life's pain.

The compulsive wave crashes
on the beach of regret.
Swearing off, we
commit to doing it
better next time.

Another ride on the
not-so-merry-go-round
begins again and again

until the wrapping unravels a little
and we open to letting Presence in;
just a little space for merciful curiosity Now,
gently polishing the mirror of the heart.

Illusive, Slippery Shame

inner driving force
says I am faulty;
mentally fixates on needing
life to be different,

projects,
asks world
to show Little Me
how to be
more fully alive,
the joyous one.

Somehow escape is at hand
from mind-made prison of self.

Who cannot face the pain
of being human and polishes bars?

Who whispers and shouts,
"try this, buy that,
if she would only do this,
take a vacation?"

Who runs to mirages in the desert?

Time slips away.

Shame attracts more
in the house swept clean;
dwelling in dark corners,
inviting shady characters to join,
trusting the untrustworthy,
confessing, drawing condemnation,
hope beyond hope
that it will be different next time

while seeking love in pain.

Young man cries
through layers of time,
"I wanted so badly to be loved."

Inner monster
no one can love,
hair covered, back arching,
mouth gaping,
fangs protruding, pleads
for acceptance.

Life was a movie seen
through dust-covered
metal screens
filled with bugs
while dragging grief-laden
ball and chain.

Allowing, seeing,
feeling, hearing,
loving monster,
prison bars fall away,
demons morph,
sins are forgiven.

Pick up the mat and walk.

We were having a discussion at Starbuck's about
foster children and severed spiritual bonds. So it was
with me and my journey to the British School—Mom,
Dad, brother, sister and me. I felt and heard ethereal
flesh ripping and chords popping: so many loose ends
searching for new attachment.

There is an opening in this early pain and suffering.

Black Purse

In that night of terror after news of lost work,
mind shouted, "This is the beginning of
the end."

I saw black shoulder harness across my
breast
holding black purse snapped tightly shut.
In thin place between waking and sleep,
I knew it as shame banked for decades.

Musical hands of guides and angels
reached to lift this burden, and
yet my mind held the purse
strapped across the breast.

I prayed the way I do not want to,
"Help me."
Hands thrust in and loosened the belt.
I saw light.

I asked for help for the firm; they withdrew.
"It is you we are here to help;
the rest will be taken care of."
Easy hands permeate, offering
acceptance in the human family.

They knew it would be long after the fall
before we could face the abuse,

hardening and filling purse with shame
that blames and asks "Why?"

only to learn decades later that "why" is
not a helpful question.

Severed bonds searched
so many false connections;
all along connectedness
was as close as breathing.

Rage

exploding,
rises relentlessly,
demands to engulf
and spew fireworks in
teeth-gnashing frustration.

Trumpets scream.

Life thwarted in manipulation and neglect,
children raising children,
spawned rancor and oblivion
in unfulfilling desires and distractions and
construction of fortresses of arrogance
to protect the pain.

Day after day
phantom beasts return
threatening to devour.

There is no way out,
only through

facing the terror of
gargoyles at the gates of
deep primordial fear;

standing in the storm of
quaking disturbance,
drenching winds and
bitter rain pebbles;

watching guns, flurry of fists,
mind directing
murderous righteousness,
domination and
denial of inner desperation;

curiously feeling without judging
urges to cast out, reject, turn our backs;

hearing without condemnation
harsh words of blame and shame;

opening heart to seeing shadow boxing;

and welcoming
with warmth and patience
hurting inner little ones
calling only for Love,
wanting to be seen,
and to join and sustain
the journey home.

In awareness of inner eternal
immutable goodness and
peace fully felt,
fists open,
defenses fall away to
reveal vulnerability,
weapons drop.

Desire II

Floating between waking and sleeping,
inquiring into darkness,
I heard the shaming voice.

(Big Surprise!)

"How could you buy that?
You can't afford it!"

I saw and felt deep holding
of desperate tiniest entity
deep in the basement
cringing with the words
"you don't deserve,"

translating to
no merit and
underserving
of anything good:
nice clothes or
maternal embrace.

Stepping outside,
moving barefoot
on the rain-soaked grass,
feeling energy flowing,
tears ran on the cheeks,
groans spontaneously exited
into the wet winter morning.

Gathering,
I welcomed this tiniest little entity
to open heart where
you deserve all there is,
dear one,
so much more than you can imagine.

It is ok. I am here for you.
you are safe NOW.

Such relief in knowing
that havoc-wreaking desires
originate in the muted and
poorly translated messages
and unexamined beliefs of
a locked-down dear one
wanting only to come home.

Welcoming this we do for all.

Evening Meditation

Entering inner stillness
deep in abdominal contraction,
I glimpsed body's fluids surging like
turbid red brown milky storm waters
laden with soil washed from the land,
tumbling and rising, seeking to over-top
constricting banks and find restful liberation
on the evenness of the easy floodplain
of pure awareness.

Amid tissue collapsing,
little voice in the void,
deep in buried cistern,
in soft desperation called,
"I am dying."

Observing mind tightened like a fist,
clinging like lint to what it knows,
I need this hurt to be whole,
I surrendered to fluid gurgling
releasing violent coughing,
constricted visceral throat shouting
from ages past.

Tears flowed to cool and soften.

At the window, mocking birds chirped.
Staccato twilling joyously announced
new life unfolding as golden clouds ushered
sun behind the mountains.

This visit to inner terror is not
for the reason I think (it never is):
business seemingly
on the brink of collapse.

Terror of Life itself stored for lifetimes,
non-distinct and anonymous, dwells
next to thoracic angelic loveliness;
Presence desiring wholeness and merciful
exploration to gently bring hurt to light
to become light.

They encounter like reluctant lovers
stealing away to rest blindly in embrace
achingly longed for, penetrating deeper
into releasing the tightened grip
of resisting mind,
one finger at a time,
to open-hearted spaciousness where
all opposites coincide in the One
and merge into the Essential.

In a Waking Moment

within a dream
in depth of silence and
wilderness of sleep,
a woman spoke in the circle of ten
of likelihood of a dreaded disease:

Leukemia (extreme cultural anemia).

It was Dad's final diagnosis.

What is truly needed?
Look and explore.

Body tightens in irritation;
windows and doors close.

Deep core held defenses,
armored to protect vulnerability,
squeeze and thwart inspiration;
Little Me asks: "Why bother?"
I will do what I want when I want.
Deep holding requests mercy.

Attempts to control Life,
following old ways
driven by old ideas;
offer enormous mercy.

Isolation in work world,
so much mental harshness
obscuring transcendence,
offer mercy.

Deep twisted desire for fraternal acceptance,
offer mercy.

Chest-held tired, aching grief desires rest in
Mercy

while mind wants more doing and resisting.
Let thoughts float on merciful
heart spaciousness.

Holdings of lifetimes,
paintings not painted,
poetry and prose unwritten,
fruit not born or harvested,
love and creativity unexpressed
hide in cramped inner stagnant space.

Un-kissed imagination takes its revenge
for being slighted.

Press, breathe deeply into heart incrustations
offering whispers of mercy;
this is our Infinite Nature.

Stolen Identity

Insidious cultural maleness is suffering.
Vulnerability, fragility, emotions disallowed,
femininity and joy spurned.

Impatience abounds, huffing, puffing,
gotta go,
need to function like clockwork.

Quiet time-bound deadness,
rightness and tightness
cover "Little One's" grieving
lost identity confiscated by giants
who smothered and rejected.

Giants showed us we were wrong, shouting,
"Sissy, fagot and girl," and most everyone
looked like a giant threatening to disapprove
of what we know deep within as joyously true.

Left-brained harshness created his-story;
one damned thing after another became
my story;
tunnel vision obscuring deep heart-felt
mystery.

Deep rage wants to make giants pay,
seeks to become giant,
and covers fear of those
who remind of past giants.

Fear and rage cover grief of deep loss.

Gently and persistently, like feather on cotton,
true nature reemerges in welcoming
all feelings to open heart that offers mercy
to giants who know not what they do.

A child shall lead them.

FLOWING HEART,
WELCOMING AWARENESS

Unpacking opens the door to flowing energy and greater Present-moment awareness. Courageously, we employ the test of stillness to assess the reality of thoughts. We are preparing to move on, know ourselves as the infinite ocean of awareness and experience the one "I am," resting in awareness. Resistance is the un-integrated child self, believing in the wrongfulness of feelings and that Life does not support. Awareness reveals the body's infinite intelligence where illusion of "me and my body" fades in the Infinite Grace of One Real Body.

We experience freedom when curiously entering feelings of confinement and separateness and watching the desperate need to escape. Surrender to binding, aching tightness reveals light shining in infinite allowing. This is not passivity. It is the power to resurrect, heal the sick, raise the dead, and speak words of truth. Moving deeper, we can face inner terror and meet Giver in dark shadows. Inner exploration allows the cultivation of the bare ground of resistance.

The Test

How do we know what is Real?

Employ the test of stillness.

Go in and in and in.

Listen.

Who is thinking?

What happens to thought that floats
on calm, deep waters and disappears?

Resistance speaks,
"Real?
Of course each thought is real."

Subject again and again.

Can we trust thoughts that remain
only a moment and so often conflict?
Are there two or one of you and me?

We are preparing to move beyond,
to know ourselves as
infinite ocean of awareness
watching and focusing with still mind
yet not separate from thinking.

Awareness sees illusion:
the double bind of confinement and
abandonment.

We are the gift of freedom
knowing the ground of Being, our root,
free to watch the reaction emanating from
illusion's identity and let it float as mind
learns to serve the heart.

Allowing

I ran barefoot on the grass,
cool of spring on my soles,
earth's caress lifting me through
each flying step,
legs straining in body's inner aliveness.

From the left came fearful chatter
about tomorrow's meeting.
Imagined betrayer would be there;
projected anger and argument arose.

I returned and knew aliveness again,
back and forth, and then I knew both
as part of the whole,
the "me" within the "I."

So strange and different,
the "I,"
caressingly held and allowed both;
resting as awareness.

Joy and Resistance

In morning meditation
I knew such joy, every cell alive, singing.
Then came resistance to joy!
Little cloud wanted tears.
The smallest thought
separated heaven and earth.

Walking to work, I saw the
white haired boy reminding
of pictures of me, not more than four,
lip curled, sobbing.

Teachers asked (told):
"You are ok, right?"
I knew him as myself.
He wanted so to be ok, but I
heard the shouting inside.

"No!
This is not ok to sit ALONE on
the concrete sobbing in pain and
giants telling me not to feel.
I need to be heard and know
Life supports me."

Day after day I see him and
open heart whispers:
"It is safe now.
Life supports our journey."

Real Body

We meditate and discover
infinite intelligence in this soul-carrying shell;
thousands of reactions and responses,
breathing, heart beating,
trillions of genius cells work together.

Ego mind with 60,000 thoughts in one day,
repeating the same "little me" story,
thinks it knows better!

Such a miracle that these vessels know
how to move, operate and bring balance
carrying so many heavy burdens of thought
and trapped childhood emotions.

We may try to trick the body with
medication, suppression and manipulation,
but it knows better
and presents invitations and invoices.

Feel earthen heaviness, denseness and solidity.
Go into body aliveness;
notice energy move and
receive subtler higher Essence.

The innocent child within each of us
relentlessly requests our attention.
Proactively and curiously accept the invitations.

Breathe each breath fully aware,
carefully and clearly, as if the
last Ahh opens into the Light,
deepest realm of Being,
with clear open heart
where illusion of me and
my body fades into the
Infinite Grace of One Real Body.

Freedom

My heart tore when confining puppies
(they love to run free),
when subjecting the girl from South Dakota
to assisted living.

Entrapment and rejection!

Illusion!?

Surrender to what is
and in this be transformed.

Crucifixion is the extreme teaching example,
dispelling the myth of confinement and
abandonment.

Difficult enough to surrender to confinement
and isolation of chair, computer, desk, email,
to this Here and Now
while "if-only" mind
searches like a wolf pack out for the hunt.

So much fatigue and suffering.

Life presents this moment to
choose to choose again.

Try what you will to get attention
and assuage feelings of aloneness,
to do what you want when you want,
to avoid feelings of confinement,
to be free.

Only one way works;
Face, feel and forgive.
Bring open heart to
where there is hatred.

Stand in earth's vibration and
accept fully the binding aching
tightness; allow belly to loosen.

Return again and again to open heart.
Spaciousness so full allows
any quality of mind
without closing.

Enter mercifully into anxiety,
that desperate need for any exit.

Freedom is in just this much
light shining in Infinite Allowing,
now uncovering what has always been.
This is not satisfying desires
or passivity.

It is power to resurrect,
heal the sick
raise the dead
speak words of truth.

Freedom II

Impending confinement triggered awareness
of suffering and pain held for decades.
"Isn't that interesting?" I mused.
"What needs to be revealed?"

Then the bear came rushing
with the 14th birthday gift a few days
after arriving at the British School.

Years ago, tears fell on an
an unsigned typewritten letter
from home sent that day;
"study hard" but no Birthday wish.

The apricot tree planted where it burned
produces sweet nourishing fruit today.

The veterans had a plan
in the dark locker room
where they held and stripped me,
had their way, and threw me
outside where girls giggled
and I shamefully covered nakedness.

Retreating into dark locker room,
in excruciating gripping aloneness,
and teeth gnashing entrapment,
mind pined for freedom.

Defensive holding to pain for decades
protected delicate juvenile
psyche from the unseen story:

"You deserved that and more because
you are such dung;
why else would your parents
send you to that place?"

"Tell me about it, dear one."
Tearfully I offered
mercy to the little one
frozen in body mind,
held by five,
unable to escape.

Even when released naked,
there was no place to go
except into darkness of the locker room,
into darkness of millennia until

such lucid and fluid freedom I found
in entering fully into
that moment's confinement
that never affected this "I am;"

into so many years spent by Little One
in blackness believing story of
wrongfulness and fighting
shadowy phantoms.

Invited Giver meets dark shadows
in secret and sacred Light.

It is the will of the One
that none of these little ones be lost.

Innocence

During the cold and darkest
days of winter,
Light is coming.

Born into this world innocent,
we come to know pain
held for generations
as friendly helper.

In the manger of the human heart
there is courageous opening
to break mind's grip,
allowing children unseen
to timidly emerge
crying, shivering and sweating.

Conceptual deep freeze
of trauma and drama thaws,
blazing a path for souls
floating on the tides of time
and body-minds striving
to assuage felt faultiness.

Innocence calls us from
across the tracks and
through the gates
to look in the street,
behind the buildings,
along the river, and see
the tents and wide eyes
asking only to be seen.

My gifts may seem small
from where you walk in finery;
smiles and gratitude arising
alongside deep belief in

"I am not enough."

This is all I have. Please see me.
Taste and see immutable goodness
of the holy child within.
This is our time of innocence.

Mary of Bethany

Sister Martha busy with divided doing,
wanting approval, admonished passivity.

Master 's words,
"Mary chose the better part,"
ring true across millennia,
ever shining as Essential
among attention seeking
mind-made options.

Still and alive companioning
Presence purifying heart for service;
this will not be taken from us.

For Mary, following the way
of inner stillness and undivided heart,
poured out perfumed sweetness
onto the Master.

Fragrance filled the room
as she gave herself fully
to One Life.

This indeed will be kept for all.

God's Arms

Love is for giving
without expectation.

Core misalignment draws love
masquerading fiercely
as messengers unrelenting.

Mind recoils from pain
creating more
until desperation gives way
to surrender, and falling
into God's arms
to discover courage to forgive
even the unforgivable,

to bring love where there is hate,
to relieve the heart from the clutches of
harmful acts and trauma filled past

and realize

God's arms are
our arms.

Plowing New Ground

Exposed fall soil
gently softened by October rains
is fresh as morning dew
in earthly perfume.

Stripped naked by harvest,
ground opens for cultivation before
winter rest.

Dry clay, rock hard and cracked
by summer sun, invites Plow and
Gentle Rainmaker
to dissolve blockiness
into smooth fertile ground

and touch recalcitrance
as old as alluvium
hardened by robotic emptiness
and misplaced trust.

Encased soul seeks release from
rock-hard resisting and confusion
that blocks nourishing dark richness
and leaves fields fallow and barren.

There is no other way
except through allowing
plowing of the
bare ground of existence.

One by one,
frozen memories surface,
clods dissolve to fuel Unfolding.

Lost little ones locked inside
emerge into the sea of stillness
underlying the world of form.

Time slips away for seeking at the surface
and arrives for exploring the depths
where resistance is welcomed and
released for the coming spring
deeply rooted in Being.

REMEMBER

To remember who we are beyond form is to remain alert. There are no ordinary moments. Spirit is alive in each unfolding. In every instance there is a glimmer, a whisper, eyes opening, light coming and going, Presence beholding us from the other side of the gap. Remembering arises during waking moments while experiencing the Infinite in the eyes of the beloved. Radical and merciful grace brings beliefs in the power of the past to transmute into nourishment for awakening.

Fearful voices declare separateness and unworthiness. There is opening in merciful attendance to the desperation and anger. Aggression melts and gives way to knowing that the vessel is not long for this world and felt gracious capacity and vastness of Being. Exploring, watching, feeling and listening transform separateness to grace-filled unbinding. In this is freedom to forgive and save the world.

The message of the cross is, "Teach love for this is who we are." Without full acceptance of pain and suffering as lessons Life would have us learn, there can be no resurrection. Without forgiveness (unconditional love is for giving), we cannot commend our soul to the One. Upon remembering, the story that seemed shining and true for so long unravels and loses luster. True help gathers lost lambs and dispels delusion. Inner wondrous oneness knows that all that is needed exists.

Awaken from the Fiction Coma

You know not the hour or the day
when light will come.

Remain in alert stillness watching
within and without,
for in every moment
there it is, a glimmer,
a whisper, eyes opening,
light coming and going.

Awaken, there are no ordinary moments.

Spirit is alive in each unfolding.

Retreat not to sleep after the test
(I am glad that is over)
deluded that everything is under control,
only to be blindsided again by monsters that
come to devour just as things are coming
together again.

All has a time and a place.
Life offers what is doable now,
no more, no less.

Required change will become clear and
doors will effortlessly open.
No need to push the river upstream.

Remain awake—
there are no ordinary moments.

Forgetting

Upon awakening, I stretch,
sit, remember and know
the peace that passes mind-made attempts
to assign reason.

Dog barks and leaf blower hums
and mind wants all noise to stop.

Can I allow this be as it is?

Yes, serenity in this suchness,
barking, leaf blowing,
mind's reaction floating
in merciful awareness.

Hours pass and I forget
that Light has come
and world is forgiven,
in the midst of mind stuff
and computer drawing me in
until...
a waking moment in
my beloved's eyes
beholding the shared infinite
on the other side of the gap,
struggling mind stuff floats.

Ah yes, there it is, the aching
alive heart space reminding of Home.
This is my abode, simple, alert.

Peter's Dilemma

We swear off and promise
not to drink, eat too much, lie,
betray those we love
or explode in anger,
to do life better next time.

We white knuckle, resist, shun, sequester.
Suppressed little ones push back, rebel and
join in
the coup d'état.

Cock crows to awaken us
on the beach of self-loathing after
riding the compulsive wave.

So it was for Peter,
extreme teaching example.

Denying the Master three times,
he awoke to bitter truth
and wept in wrongfulness.

Yet after fleeing
flock and shepherd,
retreating to old ways,
Master,
seeing past
illusion of unworthiness
to vast capacity
commanded:
"Feed my sheep,"
three times!

Shame is a stranger to the fallen
child learning to walk.

Radical and merciful Grace brings
deeply held belief in power of the past
to transmute to nourishment for awakening.

This is the rock,
certainty where Life rests.

Garbage?

I heard a voice speak,
desperate and angry,
"You are such dung."
surging at any mistake
past or present
or in imagined future.

Exploring,
offering merciful words:
"I see you."
Aggression melts and
whimpering whispers,
"It is my greatest fear that
I will be no more and that
I am truly dung, no more
than a disposal problem."

Here is an opening.
Surely the vessel is not long
for this world.
This earthly experience is over quickly.

Disintegration terrorizes "Little Me."

I smile in seeing the story
that opens
to suchness of freedom,
gracious capacity and vastness of being.

No Place

Juxtaposition prompted
guardian to cover the unspeakable
held by Little One as truth.

Deep in the lower back,
ball of tight flesh
protects from
"I have no place."

The business deal
(no place there),
lingering displeasure in work
(no place here),
remembering boarding school
(no place there or at home),
clearing mother's apartment
(home foundation swept away)
all stirring the "little one" deep
in the tan t'ien under watch of the guardian
that squeezes and grips.

It is the play of Life.

It was Yom Kippur,
holy day of atonement
when we packed mother's things.

Placing clothes into black plastic bags,
I felt her in each one,
always trying to look pretty.

In holding the wedding ring
with my father's name inscribed,
I felt her excitement of that day,
blissful anticipation of
living happily ever after.

She adored, I imagine,
his youthful vigor and ambition.

She believed, I imagine,
he would care for and protect,
fulfilling under strong wings.

Within a few feet lay manila folder
with divorce papers;
division!

Child custody, support documents,
my father's writing, numbers dividing,
breaking her heart,
I imagine.

She continued to look for safety
and wholeness he might have offered;
anger covering despair and
belief in unworthiness,
I imagine.

So much light in wide eyes
now dimmed by unceasing
desire to please and fear of rejection.

In brokenness, body protected
and deleted access to memories
to alleviate stress of belief in,
I imagine,
"I have no place."

Exploring again and again,
sitting with tightness from then
present now
at edges of relaxing and tightening,
Tears and voices flowed,

"I have no place."

Over and over, I heard
and stepping out of
guardian and Little One's words,
watching, feeling
this essence flowed into new vision.

"I have no place" transformed to
liberated desperation,
grace-filled unbinding, and
a place in the Open Heart.

For the wise one possesses
no pretentious honor, dignity,
family, country and no place to lay his head;
only Life to live fully Now
and trust Essence is enough.

In this is freedom to forgive,
and save the world.

Middle Way

The heart seeks the middle way
in the midst of mental noise,
anxious, wanting and not wanting
to fight and argue,
desiring the me way,
grasping at thoughts sailing on
the river of Life,
trying to show
imaginary brother and sister
how good the "me" is.

Going deeper is to feel the twinge
and sting of the little misguided
child self, powerless
to take away the sin of the world,
but desperately trying through manipulation,
anger, pleading and victimhood
to bring peace among humans.

The middle way now opens widely
to bring all into Infinite Great Reality;
the dark, luminous, peace-filled void
where I know "I am."

It is the pearl of great price
where flowing open heart
welcomes all.

Teach Love

is the message of the cross,
for love is who we are.
There can be no resurrection
without full acceptance of pain
and suffering as lessons
Life would have us learn.

Forgive for they know what they do.

Without forgiveness of our imprinting now,
we cannot commend our soul to the One;
without forgiveness of misguided searching
for Love,
there is no surrender to this here and now.

Avoidance of pain and clear mind
cannot coexist.

Without clear mind and open heart,
just for this moment,
there can be no New Life.

Abundance

Inner wondrous Oneness
knows
all that is needed exists;
the totality offers itself
in this very moment.

Beyond mind's clinging to scarcity,
there is no limit to what can be attained.

Resistance cries,
"Not enough;
I cannot."
The now small Essence
that sees illusion
surfaces and grows
as division dissolves.

All things seen and unseen
are imaginable and attainable.

Attainment is not the goal.
Waking is.

Wake and realize
there is no need
to strive and toil
in allowing flow
of grace-filled abundance,
as all things arise from and return to
silence, stillness and invisibility.

Watch and enjoy the play.

RETURNING

The journey home is through loving our resistance taken on through cultural conditioning that says accomplishment is the way to receiving unconditional love. Offering words of mercy to resistance opens the gate. Alchemist calls grief from hiding to heart's open window where it learns to trust the Caller. Little Ones cautiously emerge from invisibility as, little by little, they begin to trust mercy freely offered.

A still small inner voice says, "I want only to come home." Clear the path. Holding to pain blocks the way. Breath breathes liberation to roots of separation and tissue softens and receives. Cosmic forces that are akin to raging flood waters, volcano explosions, quaking earth and roots of the giant sequoias gently push and pull humans towards cooperation. Life prompts with images and soul responds with music and dancing.

Now is the time to dance barefoot and know Earth's longing to caress human feet. Now is the time to awaken to aliveness surging and embrace naked returning to Source. We come full circle through boarding school, homesickness and slumber of retakes to arrive where we began, awake. Now is the time to live joyfully in the will of the One. Heart beats in the hush of heaven, and breath breathes in love of Being.

Holding to Illusion
and Loving Resistance

He was named most valuable
on the college team,
and hid the large trophy in embarrassment
from those who might judge him:
"just a jock,"
as he so wanted the approval of
the enlightened.

The trophy stood on the mantle
in disintegrating home where
he was mostly not or invisible;
parents caught in pain.

Lost in the belief that no matter
what he accomplished,
it was not enough;
driven by emptiness to
accomplish more.

Just this one more thing,
then I will rest.

Little ones took on
the military industrial complex
during the go-go years.

One day a path opened
revealing grace-filled way forward
through loving resistance.

Steel Heart, Sweetheart

Boy of steel
with rippled hard muscles,
a hero fleeing feelings
protects a fragile,
juvenile psyche.

Heavy cage with polished bars
binds heart and soul.

A path opened and
Grace freely given
in light shining
through a fissure in the
military industrial complex,
exposed sobbing in unworthiness,
 "so much wrongfulness."

In the gap,
I loved that blind resistance
and devouring me-mind
and offered,
"Oh sweetheart,
we do the best we can."

It is not easy to see
the defensive game that
desires release for
the journey home
and offer love it craves.

The world's play is here for
our mercy and awakening.

Grief

comes
building,
mingling,
meandering,
grabbing,
as if once again
preparing for the journey
to boarding school.

My beloved prepares to leave,
packs, repacks and runs errands,
and this friend rises to tears, sobbing
in the contorted face.

And oh the fatigue,
as mind barks,
"Cannot face this."
and seeks sleep
while silent heart
watches and allows.

Finger touching chest,
a window opens to receive
grief
refreshing.

Alchemist

calls grief from hiding to
heart's open window
to grant grace to all.

Moving through
tortuous pathways,
grief slowly learns to trust
the Caller
softly speaking,
"Return home now,"

from the corner where
with backs to the wall and
herded like animals
we took on solidity
of anger and violence
and beliefs of unworthiness
and aloneness.

Once numbed by oblivion,
grief fiercely wakes and weeps
seeking Oneness.

Step back, look in and feel
undefended chest
offering mercy to so much
holding.

Bittersweet grief,
fully felt,
releases sweetness
through heaviness
like rays of sunlight crack open
the frigid and clouded winter sky.

Breath breathes slightest

softening to anvil-tight belly;
Presence in the midst
of unbearable pain.

Beauty and wonder beheld
point to inner fullness.
I am not alone.

We now know enough
to invite terror
to transmute
into pure awareness.

Invisible

Hidden wide-eyed deep in the visceral forest,
children hope to be seen, and fear
they will remain invisible to elders
caught in the trinity of movement,
noise and form that obscures innocence
and trust in Life's wildness.

What have we done so wrong
to remain unseen and discounted?

Beliefs of wrongfulness carried for so long
and grieving of a lifetime
desire to emerge.

A little boy so desired Daddy's attention,
he worked and imitated at Life's workbench,
desperately hoping for nourishment.
So he hunkered down
into striving and achieving,
but could not seem to satisfy Daddy.

One adult day he offered advice to engineers
that surely they would reject,
but surprisingly accepted.

In spaciousness of sweet bitterness of success,
a tiny voice said "Are you proud now, Daddy?"
and, oh, the silent sobbing from mouth
gaping while still holding the phone.

I listened, felt and pressed into the heart,
offering legitimacy to the Little One holding
desperately to illusion that the next
accomplishment would be enough to then rest.

Thank you for courageously trusting and
emerging.

Rainy Day

Inner stark landscape desires exploration;
desperation in second places
of quasi greatness;
almost first, almost wealthy, almost famous,
almost witty, almost popular,
almost handsome;

inner emptiness of almost-good-enough,
if only this or that done differently.

Focus lacked in seeking something else:
distractions, compulsions, divided heart,
deep inner knowing we are responsible
for quality of our experience,
and achieving can never fully satisfy.

Timidly I choose the second-place path,
exploring the wilderness
of 1,000 clues emanating
from Truth undivided.

Still Small Inner Voice

says, "I want only to come home."

Clear the path.

Holding to pain blocks the way;
ancient aching in the backroom
like a bitter old man rocking
in the chair of self-pity,
selling the world his distress,
meanwhile creating more.

I see and honor;
your pain is mine.
You have dwelled in my house
for many years, hidden.

Welcome to the Heart
where suffering dissolves.
It is time to come home.

Watch and embrace
unspoken words arising;
feel hands on the plow
now;
dwell not on his story.

Breath breathes liberation
to roots of separation;
tissue softens and receives.

Rebirth

Anger surges.
Watch.
Feel.
Who is afraid?
What do you fear?

I will die and life is too hard.

The victim trudges in the mire of sleep,
holding to what he wishes were not true.

Seemingly powerful until seen and
a path emerges through blame
that tries to protect the little ones
cowering inside the stiff front
facing slamming doors and verbal shrapnel;

fear to be born into the unborn,
of being hurt again.

Look and listen deeply to the calm knowing
of safety in the gentle stroke of mercy
in outstretched hands.

Eyes wide with fear soften in "all is well;"
rebirth into the unborn
through perfect safety;

still alert awareness emerging through
fearless infinite allowing
crossing the chasm of fear
to offer courage to a thin and fragile shell of
resistance.

Cosmic Forces Are At Work

Life requests merely cooperation
and attention to the emerging vision
of light shining from assembling puzzle
pieces.

You belong to this One Life.

Cosmic forces far greater than mind can
fathom,
like raging flood waters, volcanoes,
quaking earth and roots of giant sequoias
gently and mysteriously pull
and push humans to cooperate.

Forces of love are like gravity;
vast, invisible and unstoppable.
No amount of thinking can arrest;
better to allow and surrender,
unbinding souls from mind's barrenness.

Fearfully, we cannot resist.

Visceral knowing grants courage
to face that from which we retreated.

Forlorn little ones buried in time ask
for heart's merciful reassuring voice.

Receiving, soul responds
with music and dancing.

Light reveals home never departed.

Stand then Dance Again

Mental body wants to run from
overwhelm of manipulation and drama,
in the midst of deep strain held
in the bowels and loud mental turbulence.
Legs tighten, grow brittle and crumple.
Heart withers resisting pain.

Feel and remember humans' lost art;
joyously and wildly running free
and dancing barefoot on the Earth.

Mental story repeats, I just want to be free
but me-mind can't face the answer:
stand steadfast in smelly discomfort,
allow reconciliation
while heart courageously offers mercy
and warmly hugs what is hidden.

How can we be whole if we shun
that which longs for release to shine
and light the pathway to wholeness?

How can we truly dance again
before we learn to stand?

Join with pain and go beyond to
enter truth of living Life directly.

Homecoming

Now is the time to dance barefoot and know
earth's longing to caress human feet and
breathe Earth's breath.

Now is the time to awaken
to aliveness surging and
embrace naked returning
to Source.

We come full circle through boarding school,
homesickness and slumber of retakes
to arrive where we began,
awake.

It is Adam's journey through
restless judging and labeling where
heart hardened in separation,
to the garden to stand solidly on even soft
muscle of the land and musically
delight in singing vines whispering,
"Now is the time to live joyfully
in the will of the One."

Open heart beats joyfully
in the hush of heaven, and leaps,
welcoming prodigal mind returning
from endless excursions to the land of time.

Breath breathes in love of Being.

Creation excitedly awaits.

A Vision of the Vein of Gold

shining brightly wedged in dark hard rock
arrived in a dream.

Friends left to prospect
and I remained with
Steward watching over who
inquired about the alchemy;
bubbling dissolution of rock
fueled by breath, revealing ever
more precious metal.

I awoke knowing this expanding
in the chest, allowing aching
homesickness to spaciously float,
graciously whispering,
"This holy instant
is the only time there is."

Let go softly again and again into
deep dark recesses of discomfort.
Behold light at the bottom of the well
and know Truth that sets us free,

free to heroically give love in return
for hatred
and bravely forgive.

Heart whispers
"Be here now,
we are never alone"

www.ingramcontent.com/pod-product-compliance
Lightning Source LLC
Chambersburg PA
CBHW031317040426
42443CB00005B/112